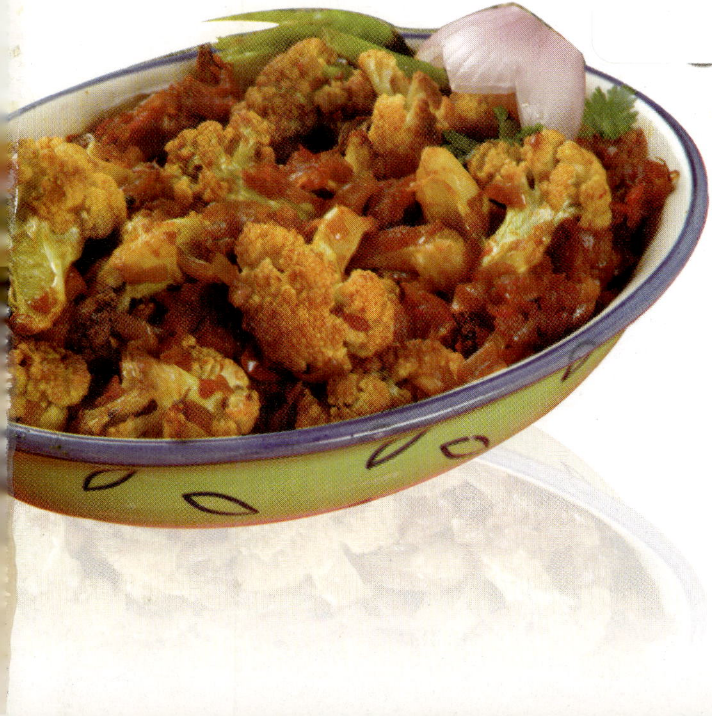

Indian
Vegetarian
Recipes

Nita Mehta
B.Sc. (Home Science)
M.Sc. (Food and Nutrition)
Gold Medalist

Nita Mehta's Indian Vegetarian Recipes

© Copyright 2008 **SNAB** Publishers Pvt Ltd

WORLD RIGHTS RESERVED. The contents—all recipes, photographs and drawings are original and copyrighted. No portion of this book shall be reproduced, stored in a retrieval system or transmitted by any means, electronic, mechanical, photocopying, recording or otherwise, without the written permission of the publishers.

While every precaution is taken in the preparation of this book, the publisher and the author assume no responsibility for errors or omissions. Neither is any liability assumed for damages resulting from the use of information contained herein.

TRADEMARKS ACKNOWLEDGED. Trademarks used, if any, are acknowledged as trademarks of their respective owners. These are used as reference only and no trademark infringement is intended upon.

First Edition 2008
ISBN 978-81-7869-214-2

Food Styling and Photography: **SNAB**

Layout and laser typesetting :

National Information Technology Academy
3A/3, Asaf Ali Road
New Delhi-110002
☎ 23252948

Published by :

SNAB
Publishers Pvt. Ltd.
3A/3 Asaf Ali Road,
New Delhi - 110002
Tel: 23252948, 23250091
Telefax:91-11-23250091

Editorial and Marketing office:
E-159, Greater Kailash-II, N.Delhi-48
Fax:91-11-29225218, 29229558
Tel:91-11-29214011, 29218727, 29218574
E-Mail: nitamehta@email.com
nitamehta@nitamehta.com
Website:http://www.nitamehta.com
Website:http://www.snabindia.com

Contributing Writers :
Anurag Mehta
Subhash Mehta

Editorial - Proofreading :
Rakesh
Ramesh

Distributed by :

THE VARIETY BOOK DEPOT
A.V.G. Bhavan, M 3 Con Circus,
New Delhi - 110 001
Tel : 23417175, 23412567; Fax : 23415335
Email: varietybookdepot@rediffmail.com

Printed by :
INDIA OFFSET PRINTERS

Rs. 89/-

Introduction

The true art of Indian cooking lies in the subtle use and variation of spices which make each dish exotic and an exciting new experience. The use of spices, however, does not mean their use in vast amounts, nor does it mean that all Indian food is extremely hot and spicy, as many people believe. The dishes can be as hot or as mild as the individual family chooses, since this is a matter of personal taste. The best Indian dishes are a clever blend of exotic spices and delicate herbs with vegetables.

Indian curries are delicious and can be prepared with just a few simple ingredients. The secret of producing these aromatic delicacies is adding the right ingredient at the right time, thus following the correct sequence of cooking.

Nita Mehta

CONTENTS

Introduction 3	The Indian Spice Box 12
Herbs & Spices 6	Some Cooking Utensils 12
Home Made Indian Spice Blends 8	Handy Tips 15

Snacks 19

Moong Dal Tilli Pakore ------- 20	Peshawari Seekh ------------------ 30
Dahi Kebab ---------------------- 23	Paneer Pasanda Tikka ---------- 32
Tandoori Bharwaan Aloo ---- 26	Palak Pakoras --------------------- 34

Curries & Dry Dishes 37

Lucknawi Koftas 38	Gobhi Fry 52
Rajasthani Gatte ki Subzi 41	Cabbage Peanut Poriyal . 55
Maharashtrian Toor Dal 44	Special Mixed Subzi 58
Paneer Makhani 46	Dum ki Arbi 60
Achaari Paneer 49	Sindhi Curry 63

E N T S

Rice, Breads & Raita 66

Nan 67
Jalpari Biryani 70
Lachha Poodina Parantha 74
Southern Tomato Rice ... 76
Baingan ka Raita 79
Beetroot Raita 82

Desserts 83

Pista Kesar Kulfi 84
Shahi Tukri Lajawaab 87
Malpuas 90
Payasam 93
Badaam ka Halwa 96

Glossary of Names/Terms 98
International Conversion Guide 100

Herbs & Spices

ENGLISH NAME		HINDI NAME	
1	Asafoetida	1	Hing
2	Bay Leaves	2	Tej Patta
3	Cardamom, Green	3	Elaichi, Chhoti Elaichi
4	Cardamom, Black	4	Moti Elaichi
5	Carom Seeds	5	Ajwain
6	Chillies, Green	6	Hari Mirch
7	Chillies, Dry Red	7	Sukhi Sabut Lal Mirch
8	Chilli Powder, Red	8	Lal Mirch Powder
9	Cinnamon	9	Dalchini
10	Cloves	10	Laung
11	Coriander Seeds	11	Sabut Dhania
12	Coriander Seeds, ground	12	Dhania Powder
13	Coriander Leaves	13	Hara Dhania
14	Cumin Seeds	14	Jeera
15	Cumin Seeds, black	15	Shah Jeera
16	Curry Leaves	16	Kari Patta
17	Fennel Seeds	17	Saunf
18	Fenugreek Seeds	18	Methi Dana
19	Fenugreek Leaves, Dried	19	Kasuri Methi
20	Garam Masala Powder	20	Garam Masala
21	Garlic	21	Lahsun
22	Ginger	22	Adrak
23	Mace	23	Javitri
24	Mango Powder, Dried	24	Amchur
25	Melon Seeds	25	Magaz
26	Mint Leaves	26	Pudina
27	Mustard Seeds	27	Rai, Sarson
28	Nigella, Onion Seeds	28	Kalaunji
29	Nutmeg	29	Jaiphal
30	Pepper corns	30	Sabut Kali Mirch
31	Pomegranate Seeds, Dried	31	Anardana
32	Sesame Seeds	32	Til
33	Saffron	33	Kesar
34	Turmeric Powder	34	Haldi

Home Made Indian Spice Blends

To perk up the flavour of Indian dishes.

GARAM MASALA
Makes ¼ cup

5-6 sticks cinnamon (*dalchini*), each 2" long
15-20 black cardamom pods (*moti elaichi*)
¾ tbsp cloves (*laung*)
2 tbsp black pepper corns (*saboot kali mirch*)
2 tbsp cumin seeds (*jeera*)
½ flower of mace (*javitri*)

1. Remove seeds of moti illaichi. Discard skin.
2. Roast all ingredients together in a non stick pan or a *tawa* for 2 minutes on low heat, stirring constantly, till fragrant.
3. Remove from heat. Cool. Grind to a fine powder in a clean coffee or spice grinder. Store in a small jar with a tight fitting lid.

CHAAT MASALA
Makes ¾ cup

3 tbsp cumin seeds (*jeera*)
1 tbsp ground ginger (*sonth*)
2 tsp carom seeds (*ajwain*)
2 tsp raw mango powder (*amchoor*)
2 tbsp ground black salt (*kala namak*)
1 tsp salt, 1 tsp ground black pepper
½ tsp ground nutmeg (*jaiphal*)

1. Roast jeera in a small nonstick pan or *tawa* to a golden brown colour. Transfer to a bowl and set aside.
2. Roast ajwain over moderate heat for about 2 minutes, till fragrant.
3. Grind roasted jeera and ajwain. Mix in the remaining ingredients.
4. Store in an airtight jar.

Tandoori Masala
Makes ½ cup

2 tbsp coriander seeds (*saboot dhania*)
2 tbsp cumin seeds (*jeera*)
1 tsp fenugreek seeds (*methi daana*)
1 tbsp black pepper corns (*saboot kali mirch*)
1 tbsp cloves (*laung*)
seeds of 8 black cardamom pods (*moti elaichi*)
1 tbsp dried fenugreek leaves (*kasoori methi*)
1 tbsp ground cinnamon (*dalchini*)
½ tbsp ground ginger (*sonth*)
½ tsp red chilli powder

1. In a nonstick pan, roast together — saboot dhania, jeera, methi dana, saboot kali mirch, laung and moti elaichi, on moderate heat for about 1 minute, until fragrant.
2. Remove from heat and let the spices cool down. Grind to a fine powder. Transfer to a bowl and mix in the remaining ingredients. Store in an air tight jar.

SAMBHAR POWDER
Makes ½ cup

¼ cup coriander seeds *(saboot dhania)*
1 tbsp cumin seeds *(jeera)*
1 tbsp, gram lentils *(channe ki dal)*
2 tsp fenugreek seeds *(methi daana)*
5-6 dry, red chillies *(saboot lal mirch)*
½ tsp asafoetida *(hing)*
1½ tsp pepper corns *(saboot kali mirch)*

1. Roast all ingredients together over low heat in a non stick pan or a *tawa*, until fragrant.
2. Cool the spices and grind to a fine powder in a small coffee grinder. Store in an air tight jar.

The Indian Spice Box

Almost every Indian kitchen has this box with various compartments to hold the basic spices & salt.

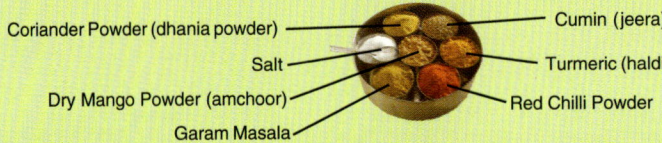

- Coriander Powder (dhania powder)
- Salt
- Dry Mango Powder (amchoor)
- Garam Masala
- Cumin (jeera)
- Turmeric (haldi)
- Red Chilli Powder

Some Cooking Utensils

Kadhai (wok) — The *kadhai* is a deep pan, round bottomed with two handles on the sides. Used mainly for frying and making Indian masala dishes. When buying one, choose a heavy-bottomed one in a medium size. Steel/Brass *kadhais* were used earlier, but now aluminium or non-stick ones are more popular. Copper-bottomed metal *kadhais* are also becoming popular.

Tawa (griddle) — A heavy iron *tawa* makes good chappatis. Buy one with a handle. These days non stick griddles are also available.

SAUCE PAN — These are deep pans with a handle. Useful for making tea, blanching vegetables in water or working with food where some sauce is needed. Usually these are made of stainless steel and are available in various sizes. Nonstick ones are also available.

PATILA (deep metal pans) — Used for boiling water, milk, rice, pasta etc. Buy a heavy-bottom one. Deep non-stick pots with handles are also available which are very handy for making soups, rice and curries.

NON STICK FRYING PAN (saute pan, skillet) — A pan about 2" high is ideal for shallow frying tikkis, kebabs and other snacks. It makes a good utensil for cooking dry/semi dry dishes too. The vegetables lie flat in a single layer on the wide bottom making them crunchy on the outside and yet moist from inside. Remember to use a plastic or a wooden spoon/ spatula to stir and fry in all nonstick vessels. Metallic ones will scratch the non stick finish and ruin it. Avoid strong detergents for washing them, warm soapy water is best. It is good to have one small (about 7" diameter) and one big (10 " diameter) pan. Dosas and pancakes too can be made conveniently in them.

KADCCHI (laddle) — Large, long - handled spoon with a small shallow bowl like spoon at the end. Should be strong enough for stirring masalas.

PALTA (pancake turner) — These broad metal turners have thin, flexible yet sturdy blade that will slide easily under the food and then be strong enough to turn the food. Not just for pancakes, it's great for turning kebabs too. Ideally choose one with a heat-resistant handle.

CHAKLA-BELAN (rolling board-rolling pin) — A marble or heavy weight rolling board is ideal for rolling out dough for chapatis, poori etc. A wooden rolling pin with it makes the set complete. Plastic rolling pins are available but I am not too comfortable with them.

PARAT (shallow bowl to knead dough) — Shallow bowl to make dough, generally stainless steel. Buy a medium size even if you are a small family, because if the bowl is too small, the surrounding area tends to get messy while making the dough. Dough can also be made in a food processor.

CHHANNI (large steel colander) — A big, wide strainer with large holes for draining cooked rice, pasta and for draining fresh vegetables after washing.

CHHARA, PAUNI (slotted spoon) — A big round, flat spoon with holes and a long handle. Good for removing fried food from oil as it drains out the oil nicely through the holes. Also used to lift solid foods out of cooking liquids.

Handy Tips

Tandoori & Other Snacks

- An oily snack is not appetizing, so make it a habit to transfer the fried snack from oil on to a tissue or a *paper napkin* to absorb the excess oil.

- A few crisp leaves of lettuce or a sprig of mint or coriander placed at the edge of the serving platter makes the snack irresistible! Make the green leaves crisp by putting them in a bowl of cold water and keeping them in the fridge for 3-4 hours or even overnight. Some cucumber slices or tomato wedges placed along with the greens, beautify it further.

- For getting a crisp coating on cutlets or rolls, dip prepared snack in a thin batter of maida and water and then roll in bread crumbs. Fry till well browned.

- A teaspoon of til (sesame seeds) or khus-khus (poppy seeds) or ajwain (carom seeds), added to coating mixture or bread crumbs makes the snack interesting.

- In the absence of bread crumbs, a mixture of ¼ cup maida and ½ cup suji may be used to get a crisp coating.

- If your cutlets fall apart, quickly tear 1-2 slices of bread and grind in a mixer to get fresh bread crumbs. Add it to the cutlet mixture for binding.
- To make crisp potato chips, soak sliced potatoes in cold water for 1 hour. Drain. Wipe dry and sprinkle some maida (plain flour) on them before frying.
- Never start frying in smoking hot oil as it will turn the snack black. Never fry in cold oil as the snack may fall apart or it may soak a lot of oil.
- For deep frying any snack, add small quantities to the oil at one time. This maintains the oil's temperature. If too many pieces are added together, the oil turns cold and a lot of oil is then absorbed by the snack.
- After deep frying, let the oil cool down. Add a little quantity of fresh oil to the used oil before reusing. This prevents the oil from discolouring.

Cooking Dal

- Soak whole pulses (saboot dals) overnight or soak in boiling water for 20 minutes, to soften skin. Use the same water for cooking in which pulses have been soaked.
- Add a few drops of oil or ghee during cooking to reduce cooking time and frothing.
- Do not use cooking soda as it destroys the vitamin B content.
- If 1 cup dal is to be cooked, add 3-4 cups water to it, depending on the type of dal.

Making Rotis/Breads

- Knead dough well and keep it covered for half an hour before using, to allow gluten strands to develop. If this is not done, its puffing quality is affected and the edges become cracked.
- Use appropriate amount of water to make the dough so that it does not become too dry or too wet in cooking. Cereals have different hydration capacity. For example, atta needs about 60 percent water (by weight) to form a soft dough for chapatis and paranthas.
- Add less water for making a firm dough for pooris and kachoris.
- Do not use too much dry flour in rolling the dough.
- Use a heavy griddle for cooking chapatis and paranthas.
- Heat ghee to smoking point before frying pooris. Later reduce flame.

Boiling Rice

- Always use good quality rice. The older the rice, the better the cooking quality.
- Wash and drain rice repeatedly until the runoff water is clear. Keep the rice soaked in fresh water for half an hour.
- For 1 cup of rice, put 5-6 cups of water to boil in a large pan . Add the rice, after the water boils. For steaming rice, use double the quantity of water. 1 cup rice will need 2 cups water for steamed rice.
- 1-2 tsp lemon juice may be added to whiten & separate the rice grains.
- When boiling rice in excess water, drain away the water as soon as the rice is just cooked. Avoid overcooking, which produces a mash. Cool in a broad vessel.
- Do not cover it. Fluff it with a fork to let the steam escape, so that the grains do not stick to each other.
- 1 cup uncooked rice will give about 2-2½ cups boiled rice.

Moong Dal Tilli Pakore

In this speciality from Delhi, paneer cubes, tomatoes and capsicums are skewered on toothpicks (tilli), and dipped in a thick batter made from moong dal to give a crusty coating when deep-fried – no wonder they are so famous!.

Makes 24 pieces

200 gm cottage cheese (*paneer*) - cut into ¾" squares, of ¼-½" thickness

1 large capsicum - cut into ¾" pieces

2 tomatoes - cut into 4 pieces lengthwise, pulp removed and cut into ¾" pieces

some chaat masala, 24 toothpicks

BATTER

½ cup dehusked moong beans (*dhuli moong dal*) - soaked for 1-2 hours

2 tbsp cornflour

2 tbsp fresh coriander (*hara dhania*) - chopped very finely

1 green chilli - chopped very finely, ½ tsp salt, or to taste, ½ tsp red chilli powder

1 tsp coriander (*dhania*) powder, ¼ tsp dried mango powder (*amchoor*)

½ tsp garam masala

1-2 pinches of tandoori red colour (optional)

1. Soak dal for 1-2 hours. Strain. Grind in a mixer with little water to a smooth thick paste. Put in a bowl. Beat well by hand to make it light.
2. Add cornflour, coriander, green chilli, salt, red chilli powder, dhania powder, amchoor powder and garam masala to dal paste. Add colour. Add a little water to get a coating consistency. Keep aside.
3. Thread a capsicum, then a paneer and then a tomato piece on each tooth pick. Keep them spaced out on the stick. Keep aside till serving time.
4. To serve, heat oil for deep frying. Dip the paneer sticks in the prepared dal batter. Shake off the excess batter.
5. Deep fry 6-8 sticks at a time till golden. Serve hot sprinkled generously with chat masala.

Dahi Kebab

Hung yogurt is thickened with roasted gram flour (besan) and shaped into incredibly light kebabs – these are carefully coated with golden fried onions dissolved in milk!

Serves 4-5

2 cups yogurt (*dahi*) - hang in a muslin cloth for 3-4 hours to drain off liquid completely

½ cup gram flour (*besan*)

2 tsp garlic paste

¾ cup oil to shallow fry

1 onion - cut into thin slices

¼ cup milk to sprinkle

DAHI KEBAB MASALA

seeds of 4 green cardamoms (*chhoti elaichi*)

½" stick cinnamon (*dalchini*)

8-10 cloves (*laung*)

½ tsp black pepper (*kali mirch*)

1 tsp salt, 1½-2 tsp red chilli powder

1. Roast gram flour for about 2 minutes till it changes colour and turns light golden. Sift the besan to make it smooth and light. Keep aside.
2. Heat oil in a frying pan. Fry sliced onions till golden brown, remove and grind to a paste. Keep fried onion paste aside till serving time.
3. Crush elaichi, dalchini and laung for dahi kebab masala. Add salt, pepper and red chilli to it. Keep masala powder aside.
4. Mix 2 tsp of the above masala powder to the hung yogurt, keeping the remaining masala powder for use in step 6. Add garlic and besan also and mix well. Divide into 20 equal parts. Flatten, wetting hands with a little water to give the kebabs smooth and even shape. Chill in the fridge for atleast 30 min.
5. Heat the oil in the pan and fry the kebabs on low heat, turning after a minute to brown both sides. Keep aside till serving time.
6. To serve, put fried onion paste in the pan on low heat. Add the remaining masala powder, stir and add the fried kebabs. Gently mix. Sprinkle milk on the kebabs, turn side and sprinkle milk on the other side too. Remove and serve at once.

Tandoori Bharwaan Aloo

What a combination! Scooped potatoes filled with paneer, almonds and thick yogurt - then baked in a tandoor.

Serves 3-4

3 big (longish) potatoes
some chaat masala to sprinkle

FILLING

3 almonds (*badaam*) - crushed roughly with a rolling pin (*belan*)
1 tbsp mint (*poodina*) leaves - chopped
1 green chilli - remove seeds and chop
4 tbsp grated *paneer*
¼ tsp salt or to taste, ¼ tsp garam masala
¼ tsp red chilli powder, a pinch dried mango powder (*amchoor*)

COVERING

½ cup thick curd (*dahi*) - hang in a muslin cloth for 30 minutes, 1 tbsp ginger paste
¼ tsp red chilli powder, ¾ tsp salt, ¼ tsp red or orange tandoori colour or turmeric (*haldi*)

BHARWAAN ALOO MASALA

1 tsp black cumin (*shah jeera*)
seeds of 2 brown cardamoms (*moti elaichi*)
6-8 pepper corns (*saboot kali mirch*)
2-3 blades of mace (*javetri*)

1. Boil potatoes in salted water till just tender. Do not over boil. When they are no longer hot, peel skin.
2. For the filling, mix crushed almonds with mint leaves, green chillies, grated paneer, salt, garam masala, red chilli and amchoor.
3. Grind or crush shah jeera, seeds of moti elaichi, pepper corns and 2-3 pinches of javetri to a coarse powder.
4. To the paneer filling, add ¼-½ teaspoon of the above freshly ground masala powder also. Keep the leftover powder aside.
5. For the covering, mix hung curd, ginger paste, remaining freshly ground masala powder, red chilli and salt. Add haldi or orange colour.

6. Run the tip of a fork on the back surface of the potatoes, making the surface rough. (The rough surface holds the curd well). Cut each potato into 2 halves, vertically. Scoop out, just a little, to get a small cavity in each potato with the back of a teaspoon. Stuff with paneer filling.
7. With a spoon apply the curd on the back and sides of the potato.
8. Grill potatoes in a gas tandoor or a preheated oven for 15 minutes on a greased wire rack till they get slightly dry.
9. Spoon some oil or melted butter on them (baste) and then grill further till the coating turns absolutely dry. Sprinkle some chaat masala and serve hot.

Peshawari Seekh

Makes 12

1½ cup soya granules (nutri nugget granules)
100 gms *paneer* - grated (1 cup)
1" piece ginger - chopped (1 tbsp)
2 green chillies - finely chopped
4 tbsp green coriander (*hara dhania*) - chopped
seeds of 4 green cardamoms (*chhoti elaichi*) - crushed or 2-3 drops kewra essence
¼ tsp mace (*javitri*) powder, optional
1 tsp channa masala
1 tsp salt, ½ tsp red chilli powder
2 bread slices - broken into pieces and churned in a mixer to get fresh crumbs

1. Soak soya granules in 1 cup of hot water for 15 minutes.
2. Strain. Squeeze out the water well from the soya granules. (No water should remain). You can also put the soya granules in a muslin cloth and squeeze.
3. Add grated paneer, ginger, green chillies, coriander, elaichi, javitri powder, chana masala, salt, and red chilli powder.
4. Churn the nutri granules alongwith all the other ingredients in a mixer till smooth.
5. Churn bread in a grinder, to get fresh bread crumbs. Add fresh crumbs to the nutri nuggets mixture. Mix well.
6. Divide the mixture into 12 equal portions and make balls.
7. Take a ball of nutri mixture and make a 2" long kebab.
8. Take a pencil or a skewer and push it carefully from one end of kebab to the other, without puncturing at any point.
9. Gently pull out skewer or the pencil. Keep the seekhs in the fridge for ½ hour.
10. Deep fry the seekhs in medium hot oil in a *kadhai* to a light brown colour. Serve hot with chutney.

Paneer Pasanda Tikka

Serves 6

300 gms whole block of cottage cheese (*paneer*) - cut into ½" thick slices
some chaat masala

MARINADE (MIX TOGETHER)
1 cup curd (*dahi*) - hang in a muslin cloth for 30 minutes
8-10 flakes of garlic, 1" piece ginger, 2 dry, red chillies - all ground together to a paste
1 tbsp oil, 1½ tsp channa masala, ¾ tsp salt or to taste
1 tsp dry fenugreek leaves (*kasoori methi*), 1 tsp lemon juice, 2-3 tbsp thick cream

FILLING
½ tsp cumin seeds (*jeera*), ¼ cup very finely chopped onion
¼ cup very finely chopped cabbage, 1 small carrot - grated finely & squeezed
½ of a small capsicum - very finely chopped (¼ cup)
4-5 cashewnuts (*kaju*) - chopped finely, 1 tsp raisins (*kishmish*) - chopped
2 tbsp finely chopped coriander (*hara dhania*)
½ tsp salt or to taste, ½ tsp chat masala, ¼ tsp turmeric (*haldi*)

1. Sprinkle chaat masala on both sides of paneer slices. Keep aside.
2. Heat 1 tbsp oil in a non stick pan or a *tawa*. Remove pan from fire and swirl or rotate it to coat the bottom with oil. Put the paneer slices on the hot pan and saute them till golden brown on both sides. Remove from pan and cut each lengthwise into half carefully, to get 2 slices from each piece. Keep aside.
3. For filling, heat 1 tbsp oil, add jeera. Stir for a few seconds. Add onion. Cook till soft. Add cabbage, carrot, capsicum, cashews and raisins. Saute for 2 minutes.
4. Add coriander, salt, chaat masala & haldi. Cook for a minute. Remove from fire.
5. Mix all ingredients of the marinade in a big shallow dish. Place a piece of cottage cheese on a flat surface or plate. Spread some marinade on one side of the paneer.
6. Sprinkle the cooked vegetable on the same side of the slice. Cover slice completely with the filling. Place the other piece of paneer on the first piece, keeping the brown side on top. Press the sandwiched paneer nicely.
7. Put the sandwiched paneer in the marinade in the bowl & turn side to cover completely with the marinade on all the sides. Keep aside till serving time in the bowl.
8. To serve, preheat oven to 180°C. Arrange the marinated paneer on a greased wire rack. Grill for 10-15 minutes till coating turns dry. Remove from oven when done. Cut each from the middle into 2 pieces. Sprinkle chaat masala. Serve hot with chutney.

Palak Pakoras

Pakoras – deep-fried vegetable fritters made with a gram flour batter – have many variations. In this recipe, batter-coated spinach leaves make a crisp and delicious snack to serve at any time of the day.

Serves 4-5

24 spinach (*palak*) leaves with 2" long stems

BATTER

½ cup gram flour (*besan*)

¼ cup semolina (*suji*)

½ tsp carom seeds (*ajwain*)

½ tsp salt, ¼ tsp red chilli powder

½ tsp coriander (*dhania*) powder

¾ cup water or as required

oil to deep-fry

1. Take spinach leaves including a little stem of about 2". Wash the spinach and pat dry on a clean kitchen towel.

2. Put all the ingredients for the batter in a bowl, adding water to make a thick batter with a coating consistency. Do not make it thin as it will not coat the leaves properly.
3. Heat the oil in a wok.
4. Dip each spinach leaf in batter so that it gets well coated.
5. Fry the leaves on medium heat, a few at a time, till golden and crisp on both sides. Remove and drain on absorbent paper towels. Serve immediately.

Curries & Dry Dishes

Lucknawi Koftas

These potato and spinach koftas are simmered in delicate gravy enriched with almonds, melon seeds and poppy seeds – a marvel of tastes and aromas.

Serves 4

KOFTAS

125 gm potatoes - boiled and mashed
¼ cup chopped coriander (*hara dhania*)
¼ cup cornflour, ½ cup chopped spinach (*palak*)
2 tbsp dry fenugreek leaves (*kasoori methi*), ½ tsp garam masala, 1 tbsp lemon juice
1 tsp salt, or to taste, oil for deep frying

MASALA PASTE

12 almonds (*badaam*), 4 tbsp melon seeds (*magaz*), 6 green chillies
4 tbsp poppy seeds (*khus khus*), 1 onion, ½" piece of ginger, 3-4 flakes of garlic

OTHER INGREDIENTS

3 tbsp oil, 2 onions - finely chopped cup yogurt (*dahi*)
½ cup milk, ¼ cup cream, ½ tsp turmeric (*haldi*), ½ cup water, 1 tsp sugar, 1 tsp salt

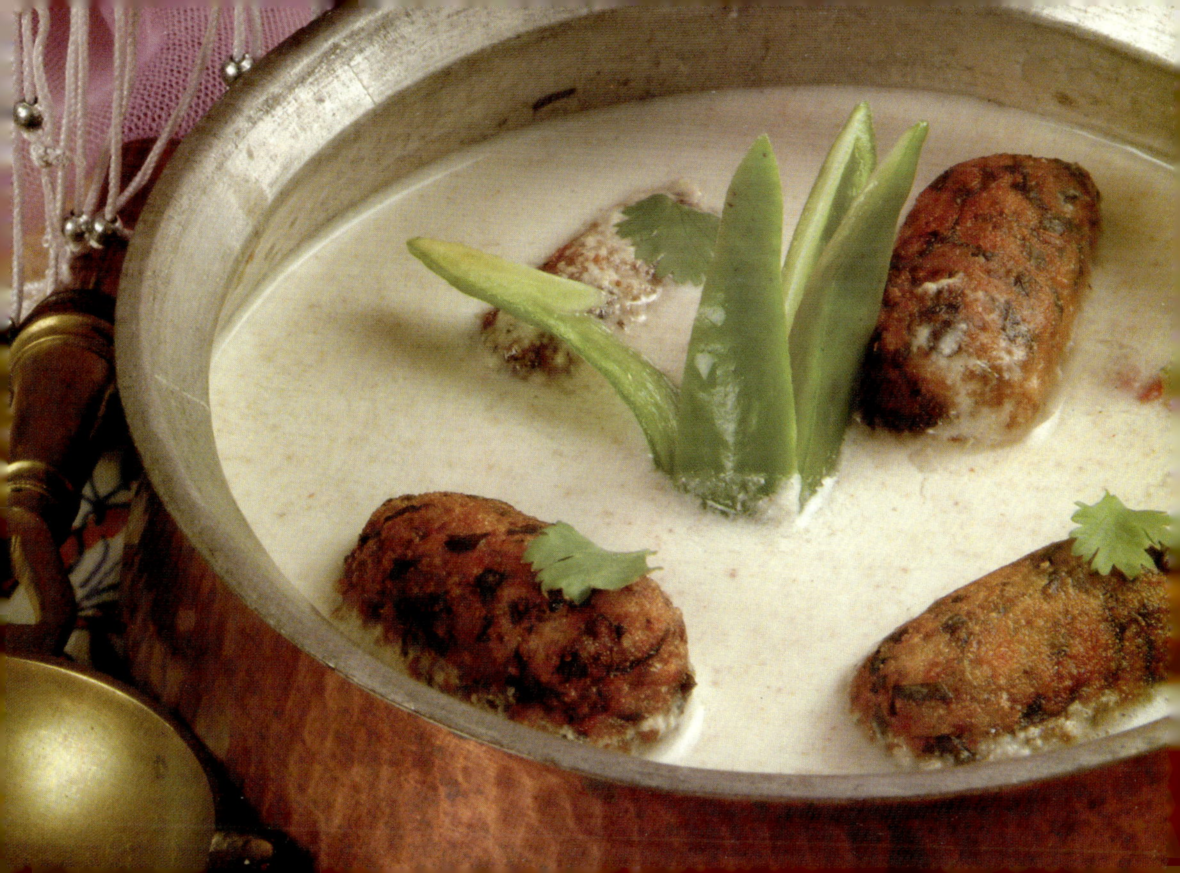

1. Mix all ingredients of the koftas together in a bowl. Form into 1½" long rolls and deep fry 1-2 at a time in hot oil and keep aside.
2. Grind all ingredients for the masala paste together in a mixer to a fine paste.
3. For the gravy, heat 3 tbsp oil add chopped onions, stir till golden brown.
4. Add the ground masala paste and fry for a 2-3 minutes.
5. Reduce heat, stirring continuously add yogurt, milk, cream, haldi, sugar and salt. Increase heat bring to a boil, stirring continuously.
6. Add ½ cup water and cook for another 5 minutes. Remove from fire and keep aside till serving time.
7. At the time of serving heat up the gravy add the koftas and simmer for a minute for the koftas to get hot. Serve hot.

Rajasthani Gatte ki Subzi

A dough made of gram flour is used to make the steamed gatte. The curry has a base of curd, gram flour and pureed tomatoes – spicy, chilli hot and brightly coloured like the place of its origin.

Serves 4-5

GATTE

¾ cup gram flour (*besan*), ¼ tsp baking soda (*mitha soda*)

½ tsp ginger-green chilli paste, ¼ tsp carom seeds (*ajwain*)

¼ tsp fennel (*saunf*) - crushed, ½ tsp salt, ½ tsp turmeric (*haldi*), ½ tsp red chilli powder

½ tsp coriander (*dhania*) powder, ½ tsp garam masala

2 tbsp yogurt (*dahi*), 1 tbsp oil

CURRY

2 tbsp oil, 2 cloves (*laung*), 1 tsp cumin seeds (*jeera*)

1 cardamom (*moti elaichi*) - crushed, ¼ tsp turmeric (*haldi*), ½ tsp red chilli powder

2 tomatoes - puree in a mixer & strain

½ tsp ginger paste, 1 green chilli - crushed

1 cup yogurt (*dahi*) mixed with 2 tsp gram flour (*besan*) & 1 cup water till smooth

1. Sift besan and soda. Add ginger chilli paste, ajwain, saunf, powdered spices and just enough curd to get a very soft dough. Mix well. Mix 1 tbsp oil and knead again. Make 4 balls. With the help of oil smeared on your hands, roll out thin fingers 3"-4" long, like cylinders.
2. Boil 5 cups of water. Keep the gatte in a stainless steel round strainer and keep the strainer on the pan of boiling water and cover with a lid.
3. Steam gatte for 5-7 minutes. Let them cool. Later cut them into rounds of ½" thickness. Keep aside.
4. For curry, blend curd, besan and 1 cup water in a mixer till very smooth. Puree tomatoes and strain them to get a smooth puree.
5. Heat 2 tbsp oil, add laung, jeera, moti elaichi, haldi and red chilli powder. Stir.
6. Add tomato puree, ginger and crushed chilli. Cook for 3 minutes till dry and oil separates.
7. Reduce heat. Add curd with besan. Stir constantly, on low heat to bring it to a boil. Simmer for 3-4 minutes.
8. Add gatte. Cook for 2-3 minutes. Serve hot garnished with hara dhania.

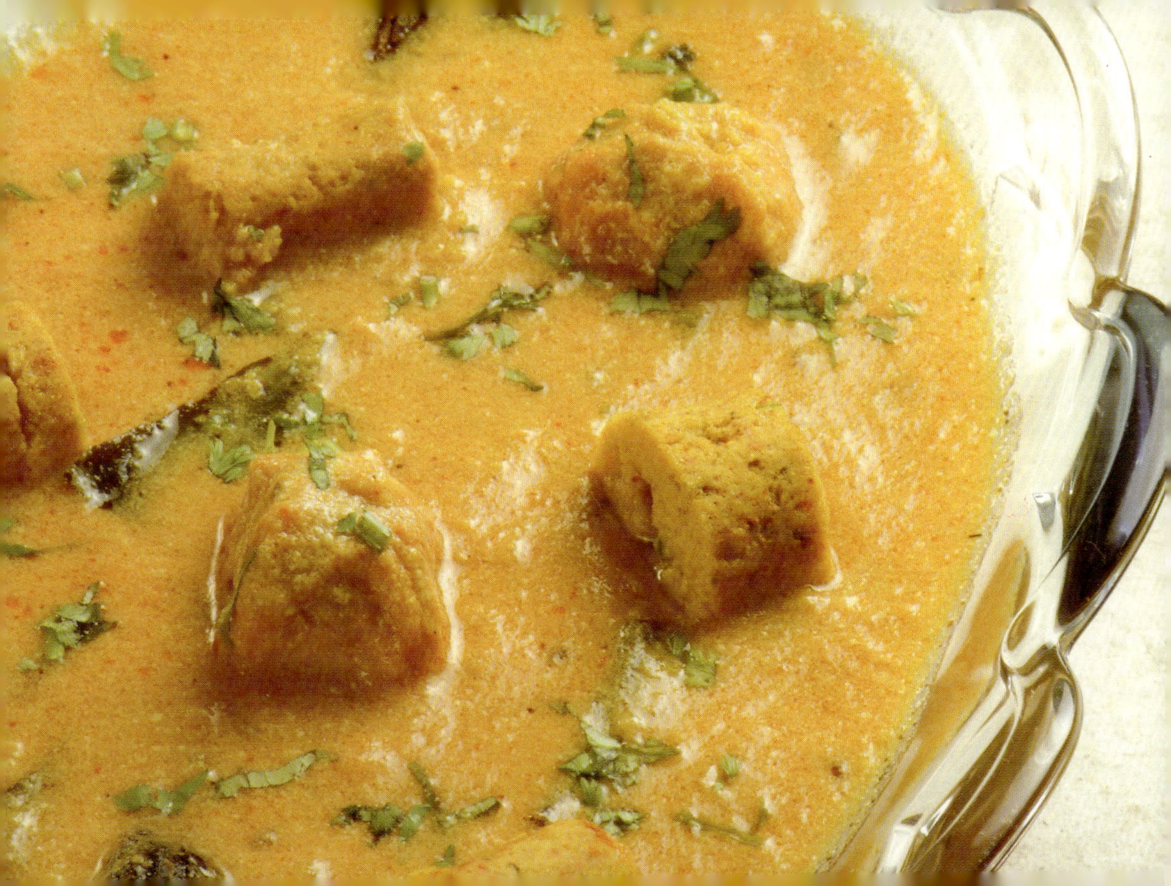

Maharashtrian Toor Dal

A touch of sweet and sour ((jaggery and lemon) gives this delicious dal the distinctive touch of the food of Maharashtra.

Serves 2-3

½ cup yellow lentils (*toor dal*), ¾ tsp salt, or to taste, ½ tsp turmeric (*haldi*) powder
1 tbsp jaggery (*gur*), 1 tbsp lemon juice, or to taste

TEMPERING/*TADKA*
2 tbsp clarified butter (*ghee*), a pinch of asafoetida (*hing*), ½ tsp mustard seeds (*rai*)
some curry leaves

1. Clean, wash dal. Soak dal in 1½ cups of water for half an hour. Drain.
2. Pressure cook dal with 2 cups water, salt and haldi on high flame till the first whistle and then simmer for 5 minutes. Remove from heat.
3. After the pressure drops, add gur and ½ cup water. Mix well. Simmer for 2-3 minutes. Remove from heat. The consistency should be thick.
4. For *tadka*/tempering heat ghee, add hing and rai. Let it crackle and add curry leaves and immediately add it to the dal. Squeeze lemon juice on it. Check taste. Serve with rice.

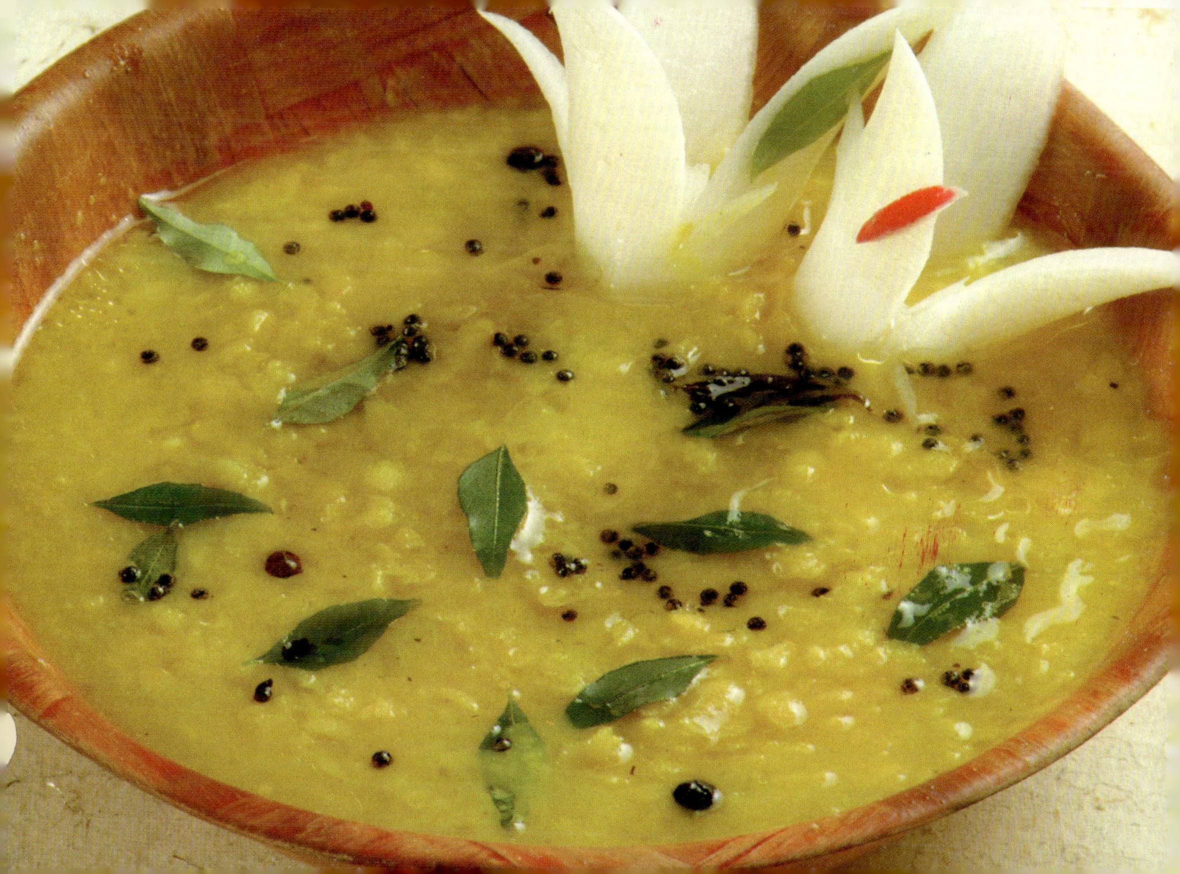

Paneer Makhani

This classic makhani gravy is created out of pureed tomatoes, butter, milk, cream and ground cashews – a paneer dish fit for a five-star banquet.

Serves 4

250 gm cottage cheese (*paneer*) - cut into 1" long pieces

¼ cup cashewnuts (*kaju*) - soak in warm water for 15 minutes

5 large (500 gm) tomatoes - each cut into 4 pieces

2 tbsp clarified butter (*desi ghee*) or butter and 2 tbsp oil

4-5 flakes garlic and 1" piece ginger - ground to a paste (1½ tsp ginger-garlic paste)

1 tbsp dry fenugreek leaves (*kasoori methi*)

1 tsp tomato ketchup

½ tsp cumin seeds (*jeera*)

2 tsp coriander (*dhania*) powder, ½ tsp garam masala

1 tsp salt, or to taste, ½ tsp red chilli powder, preferably paprika (*degi mirch*)

½ cup water

½-1 cup milk, approx.

½ cup cream (optional)

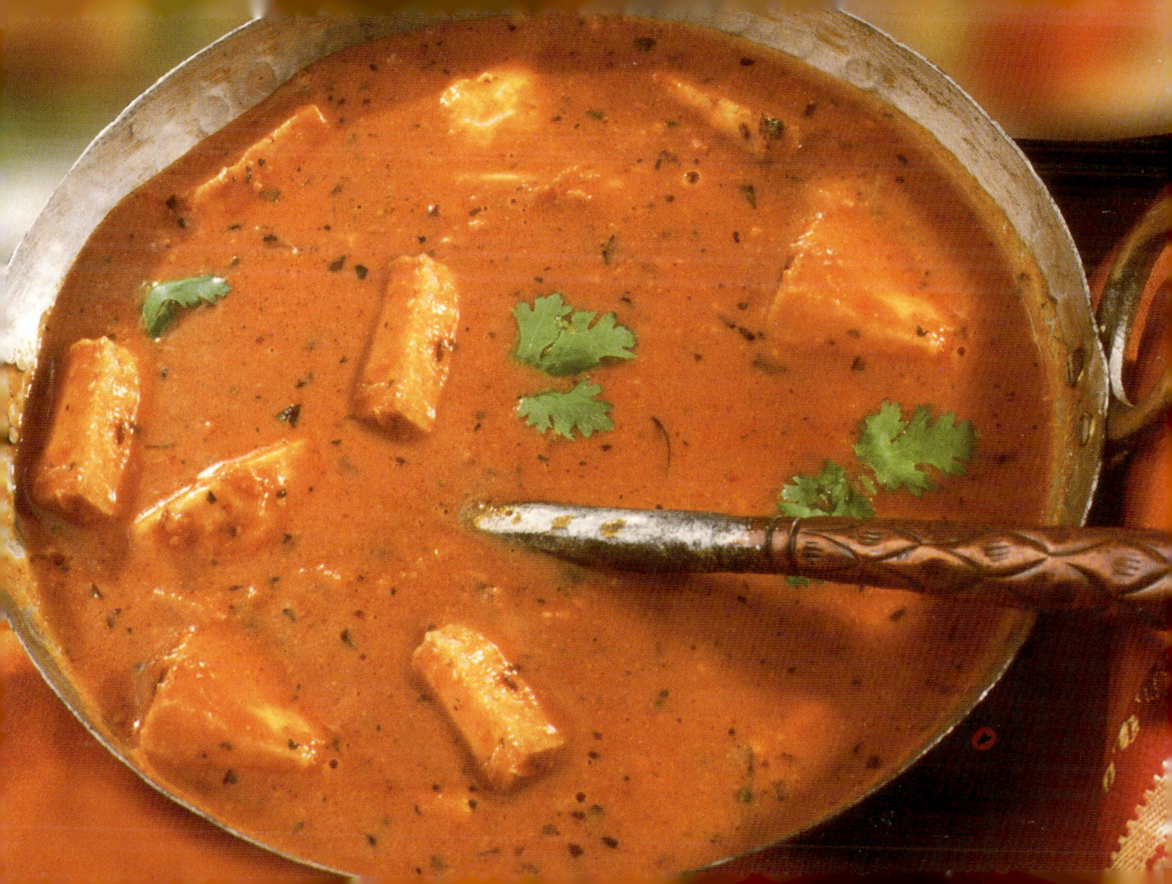

1. Drain kaju. Grind in a mixer to a very smooth paste using about 2 tbsp water.
2. Boil tomatoes in ½ cup water. Simmer for 4-5 minutes till soft. Remove from fire and cool. Grind the tomatoes along with the water to a smooth puree.
3. Heat oil and ghee or butter in a *kadhai*. Reduce heat. Add jeera. When it turns golden, add ginger-garlic paste. When paste starts to change colour add the above tomato puree and cook till dry. Add kasoori methi and tomato ketchup.
4. Add masalas - dhania powder, garam masala, salt and red chilli powder. Mix well for a few seconds. Cook till oil separates.
5. Add cashew paste. Mix well for 2 minutes. Add water. Boil. Simmer on low heat for 4-5 minutes. Reduce heat.
6. Add the paneer cubes. Remove from fire. Keep aside to cool for about 5 minutes.
7. Add enough milk to the cold paneer masala to get a thick curry, mix gently. (Remember to add milk only after the masala is no longer hot, to prevent the milk from curdling. After adding milk, heat curry on low heat.) Heat on low heat, stirring continuously till just about to boil.
8. Add cream, keeping the heat very low and stirring continuously. Remove from fire immediately and transfer to a serving dish. Serve hot.

Achaari Paneer

Pickling spices give a distinct personality – the rest of the flavours provide a harmonious balance – you will be proud of this presentation!

Serves 6

300 gm cottage cheese (*paneer*) - cut into 1½" cubes, 2 capsicums - cut into 1" pieces

¾" piece ginger & 5-6 flakes garlic - crushed to a paste (2 tsp)

1 cup curd - beat well till smooth in a mixer

4 tbsp oil, 3 onions - chopped finely

4 green chillies - chopped, ½ tsp turmeric (*haldi*) powder

1 tsp dried mango powder (*amchoor*) or lemon juice to taste, ¾ tsp garam masala

1 tsp salt or to taste, 2-3 green chillies - cut lengthwise into 4 pieces

¼ cup milk, 2-3 tbsp cream, optional

ACHAARI MASALA

2 tsp aniseeds (*saunf*), 1 tsp mustard seeds (*rai*)

a pinch of fenugreek seeds (*methi daana*), ½ tsp onion seeds (*kalonji*)

1 tsp cumin seeds (*jeera*)

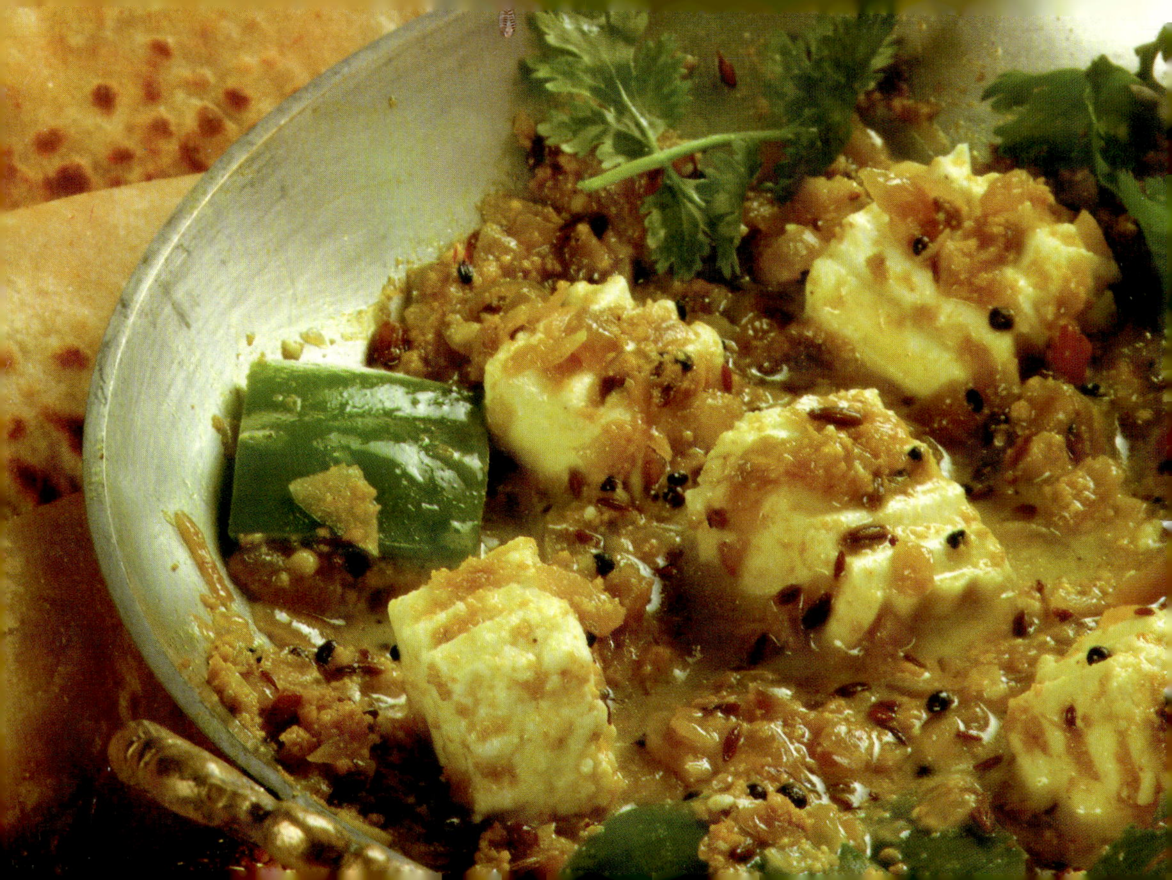

1. Cut paneer into 1½" cubes.
2. Sprinkle ½ tsp haldi, a pinch of salt and ½ tsp red chilli powder on the paneer and capsicum pieces. Mix well. Keep aside for 10 minutes.
3. Collect all seeds of the achaari masala - saunf, rai, methi daana, kalonji and jeera together.
4. Crush garlic and ginger to a paste.
5. Heat 4 tbsp oil. Add the collected seeds together to the hot oil. Let them crackle for 1 minute or till jeera turns golden.
6. Add onions and chopped green chillies. Cook till onions turn golden.
7. Add haldi and garlic-ginger paste. Mix well.
8. Reduce heat. Beat curd with 2 tbsp water and a pinch of haldi till smooth. Add gradually and keep stirring. Add amchoor, garam masala and salt or to taste. Cook for 2-3 minutes on low heat till the curd dries up a little. (Do not make it very dry). Remove from fire and let it cool down.
9. At the time of serving, add milk and slit green chillies. Add capsicum. Boil on low heat for a minute, stirring continuously. Cook on low flame for 2-3 minutes.
10. Add cream and paneer and cook for 1-2 minutes on low flame. Serve.

Gobhi Fry

Cauliflower florets tossed in a delicious masala – everyone's favourite, at all times.

Serves 4

1 medium whole cauliflower (500 gm) - cut into medium size florets with stalks

MASALA
4 tbsp oil
3 onions - chopped
seeds of 1 brown cardamom (*moti elaichi*)
3-4 pepper corns (*saboot kali mirch*)
2 cloves (*laung*)
3 tomatoes - roughly chopped
1" ginger - chopped
2 tbsp curd (*dahi*) - beat well till smooth,
½ tsp red chilli powder, ½ tsp garam masala
½ tsp turmeric (*haldi*), ½ tsp dried mango powder (*amchoor*)
1 tsp salt, or to taste

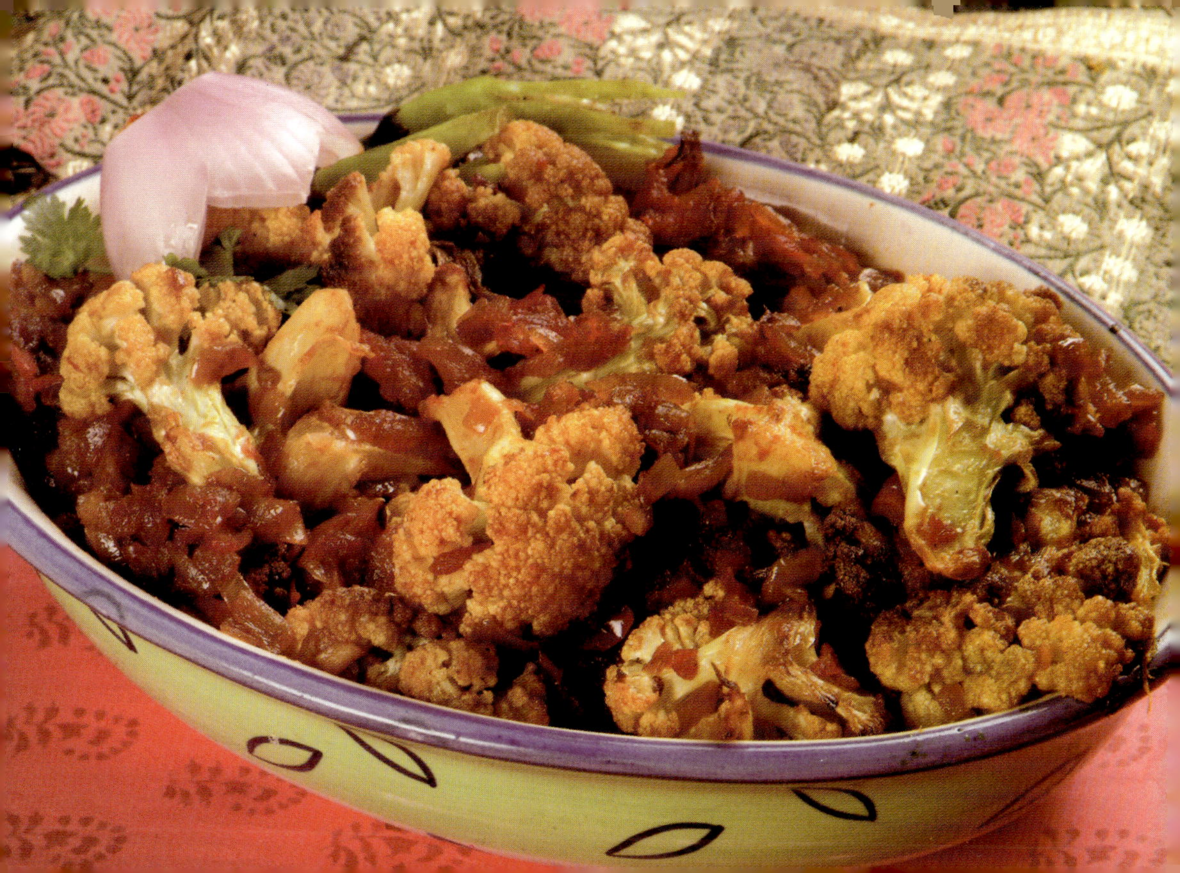

1. Break the cauliflower into medium size florets, keeping the stalk intact. Wash & pat dry on a kitchen towel.
2. Heat oil in a *kadhai* for deep frying. Add all the cauliflower pieces and fry to a light brown colour. Remove from oil and keep aside.
3. Heat 4 tbsp oil in a clean *kadhai*. Add moti elaichi, saboot kali mirch and laung. After a minute, add chopped onion. Cook till onions turn golden brown.
4. Add chopped tomatoes and ginger. Cook for 4-5 minutes till they turn soft and masala turns little dry.
5. Add well beaten curd. Cook till masala turns reddish again.
6. Reduce heat. Add red chilli powder, garam masala, haldi, amchoor and salt. Cook for 1 minute. Add ½ cup water to get a thick masala. Boil. Cook for 1 minute on low flame. Keep aside.
7. At the time of serving, heat the masala. Add the fried cauliflower pieces to the masala and mix well on low heat for 2 minutes till the vegetable gets well blended with the masala. Serve hot.

Cabbage Peanut Poriyal

A dry, spicy and crunchy South Indian side dish.

Serves 4

½ kg cabbage (1 medium) - chopped finely
½ cup peanuts (*moongphali*) - roasted
1½ tsp salt, or to taste

TEMPERING (CHOWNK)
4 tbsp oil, 1 tsp mustard seeds (*rai*), ½ tsp cumin seeds (*jeera*)
2 tsp split black gram (*dhuli urad dal*), 2 tsp bengal gram dal (*channa dal*)
2 dry, red chillies - broken into bits
½ tsp asafoetida (*hing*), ¼ cup curry leaves

PASTE (GRIND TOGETHER)
2 green chillies, 4-5 tbsp grated coconut - remove the brown skin and then grate
1 onion - chopped
1 tsp cumin seeds (*jeera*)
2 tbsp curd (*dahi*)

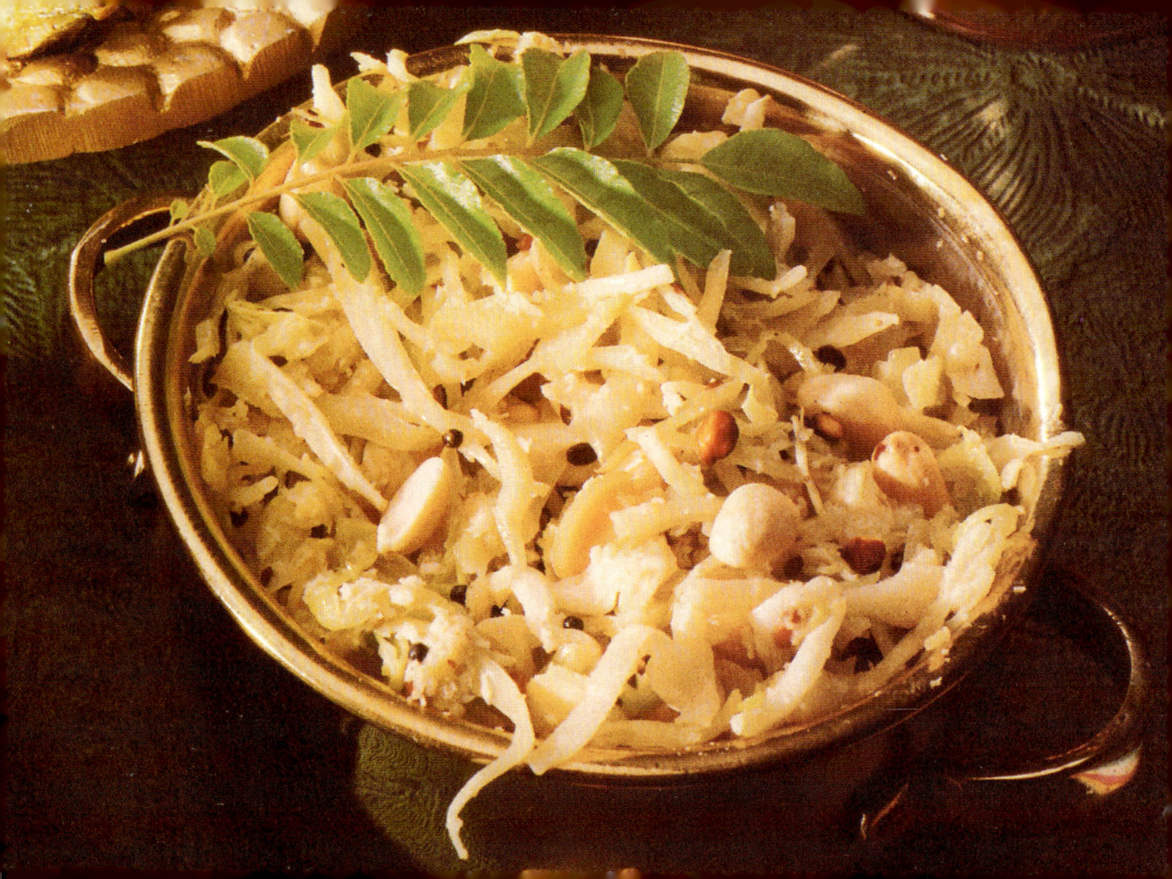

1. Heat oil. Reduce heat. Add all ingredients of tempering.
2. When dals turn golden, add the chopped cabbage. Mix well.
3. Add salt and 2 tbsp water. Mix well.
4. Add peanuts. Cover and cook on low heat for 7-8 minutes till cabbage turns tender.
5. Add the coconut paste. Stir fry for 3-4 minutes. Serve hot.

Note: You can make any poriyal in the same way - carrot, beetroot or capsicum.

Special Mixed Subzi

Serves 4

2 tbsp oil, ½ tsp cumin seeds (*jeera*), ½ tsp mustard seeds (*sarson*)
½ tsp onion seeds (*kalonji*), ¼ tsp fenugreek seeds (*methi daana*)
15-20 curry leaves, 2 onions - cut into rings, ¼ tsp turmeric (*haldi*)

MIX TOGETHER
¾ cup ready-made tomato puree, 2 tsp tomato ketchup
2 tsp ginger-garlic paste or 2 tsp ginger-garlic - finely chopped
½ tsp red chilli powder, ½ tsp dried mango powder (*amchoor*)
1 tsp coriander (*dhania*) powder, 1 tsp salt

VEGETABLES
1 carrot - cut diagonally into thin slices
10-12 french beans - sliced diagonally into 1" pieces
8-10 small florets (pieces) of cauliflower
1 green capsicum - deseed and cut into thin fingers
½ cup shelled peas (*matar*) - boiled
1 long, firm tomato - cut into 4 and then cut into thin long pieces

1. Boil 4 cups water with 1 tsp salt and ½ tsp sugar. Add sliced carrots and beans after the water boils. Boil for 2 minutes till crisp-tender. Strain. Refresh in cold water.
2. Mix together - tomato puree, tomato ketchup, ginger, garlic, red chilli powder, dhania powder, amchoor and salt in a bowl. Keep aside.
3. Collect together - jeera, sarson, kalonji and methi dana. Keep aside. Heat 2 tbsp oil in a *kadhai*. Add the collected ingredients. When jeera turns golden, reduce heat and add curry leaves and stir for a few seconds.
4. Add onions and cook till golden. Add haldi. Mix.
5. Add the tomato puree mixed with dry masalas and stir on medium heat for 2 minutes.
6. Add carrot, cauliflower and beans. Stir for 3-4 minutes.
7. Add the capsicum, peas and tomato. Stir till well blended. Remove from fire.
8. Transfer to a serving dish. Serve hot.

Dum ki Arbi

Arbi gets a gourmet image in this amazing curry, made with yogurt and boiled onion paste, thickened with poppy seeds and cooked slowly and lovingly.

Serves 4

400 gm colocasia (*arbi*)
2 tbsp poppy seeds (*khus khus*)
3 onions, 1" piece of ginger, 12 flakes of garlic
1 tsp coriander (*dhania*) powder
½ tsp red chilli powder, 1 tsp cumin (*jeera*)
½ tsp garam masala powder
1 tsp salt or to taste
½ tsp turmeric (*haldi*) powder
4-6 green cardamoms (*chhoti elaichi*)
2 cups yogurt (*dahi*)
a pinch of nutmeg (*jaiphal*) - grated
oil to deep fry
coriander leaves to garnish

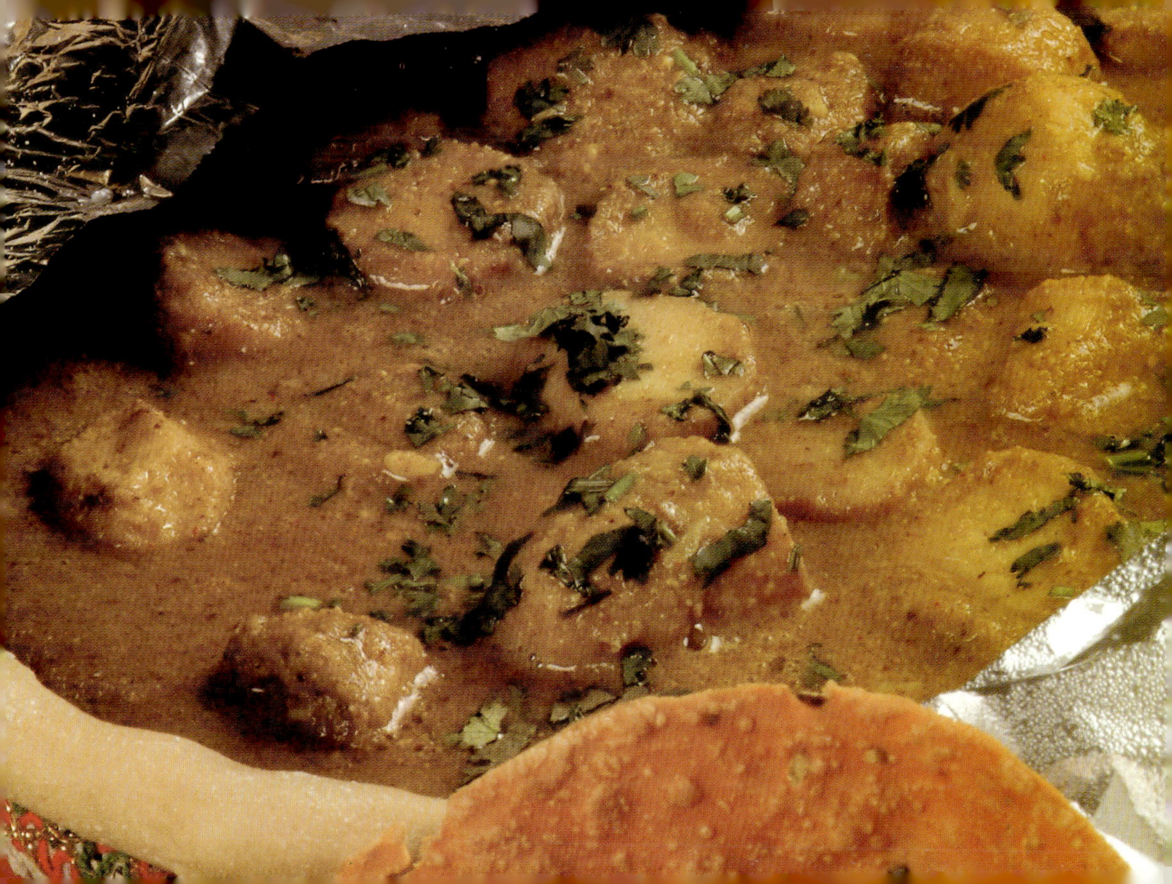

1. Soak poppy seeds in ¼ cup water. Keep aside.
2. Peel and cut arbi into 1" pieces. Deep fry in hot oil till golden brown.
3. Peel onions and cut into 4 pieces and put in a saucepan with 2 cups of water. Boil onions for 3-4 minutes till soft. Drain. Cool.
4. Grind the onion, soaked khus khus, ginger, garlic, dhania powder, red chilli powder, jeera, garam masala, salt and haldi in a blender to a paste.
5. Heat 2 tbsp oil in a pan. Add chhoti elaichi, stir for a minute.
6. Add prepared paste. Saute till light golden brown.
7. Mix yogurt with ½ cup water. Add the yogurt stirring continuously; bring it to a boil.
8. Add arbi and grated nutmeg.
9. Cover the pan with a tight fitting lid and simmer for 15 minutes. Alternatively cover the pan with aluminium foil or seal the lid with wheat flour dough, so that the aroma is trapped in the pan and does not escape.
10. Garnish with coriander and serve.

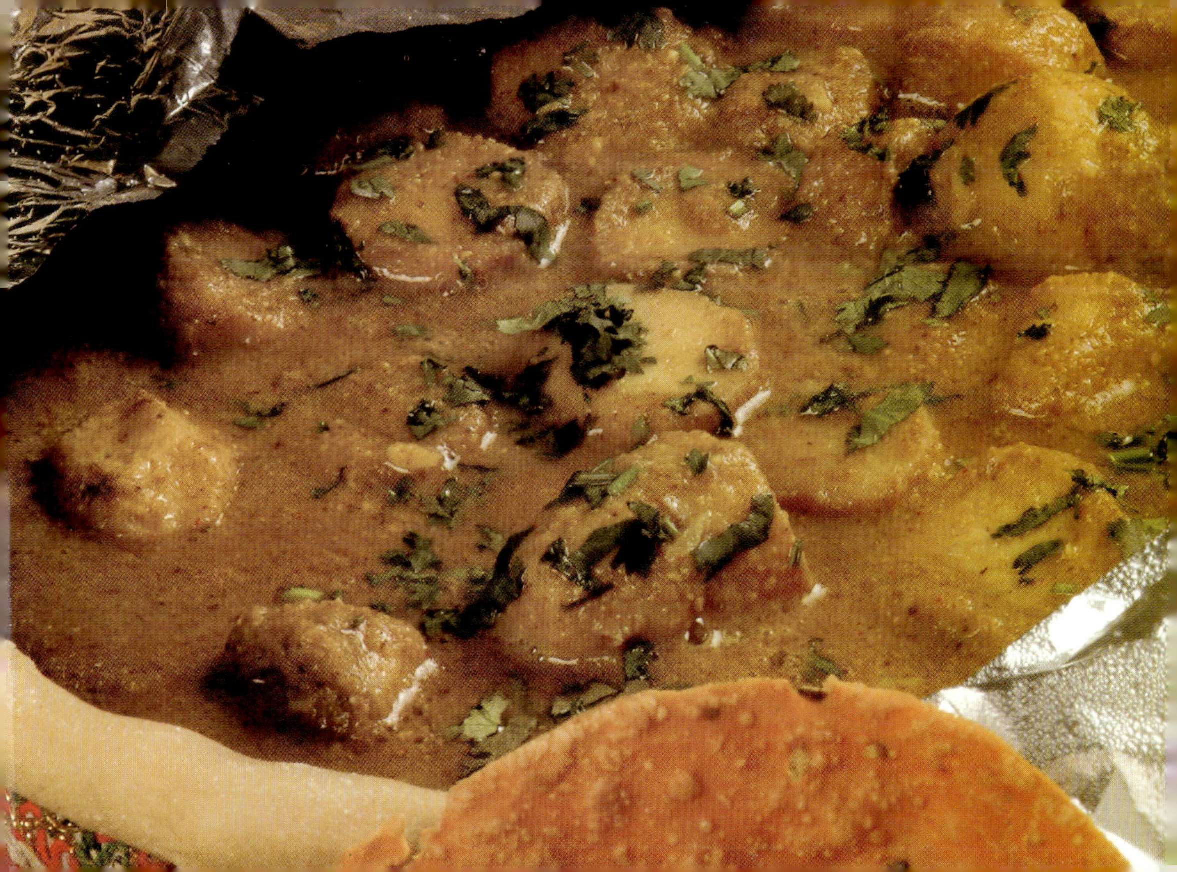

1. Soak poppy seeds in ¼ cup water. Keep aside.
2. Peel and cut arbi into 1" pieces. Deep fry in hot oil till golden brown.
3. Peel onions and cut into 4 pieces and put in a saucepan with 2 cups of water. Boil onions for 3-4 minutes till soft. Drain. Cool.
4. Grind the onion, soaked khus khus, ginger, garlic, dhania powder, red chilli powder, jeera, garam masala, salt and haldi in a blender to a paste.
5. Heat 2 tbsp oil in a pan. Add chhoti elaichi, stir for a minute.
6. Add prepared paste. Saute till light golden brown.
7. Mix yogurt with ½ cup water. Add the yogurt stirring continuously; bring it to a boil.
8. Add arbi and grated nutmeg.
9. Cover the pan with a tight fitting lid and simmer for 15 minutes. Alternatively cover the pan with aluminium foil or seal the lid with wheat flour dough, so that the aroma is trapped in the pan and does not escape.
10. Garnish with coriander and serve.

Sindhi Curry

A medley of vegetables in a well seasoned tangy tomato gravy thickened with gram flour.

Serves 4

500 gm tomatoes

3 tbsp oil

1½ tsp mustard seeds (*rai*), 1 tsp cumin seeds (*jeera*)

½ cup gram flour (*besan*)

1 potato - chopped, 8 green chillies

1 long, thin brinjal - chopped

3-4 guwar or french beans - chopped

2 drumsticks - cut into 3" pieces

10-12 lady fingers - each cut into 2 pieces & fried in oil

½ tsp turmeric (*haldi*) powder, 2 tsp red chilli powder

6 kokums or a lemon-size ball of tamarind (*imli*) - soaked in ½ cup water

2 tbsp finely chopped coriander (*hara dhania*)

1½ tsp salt, or to taste

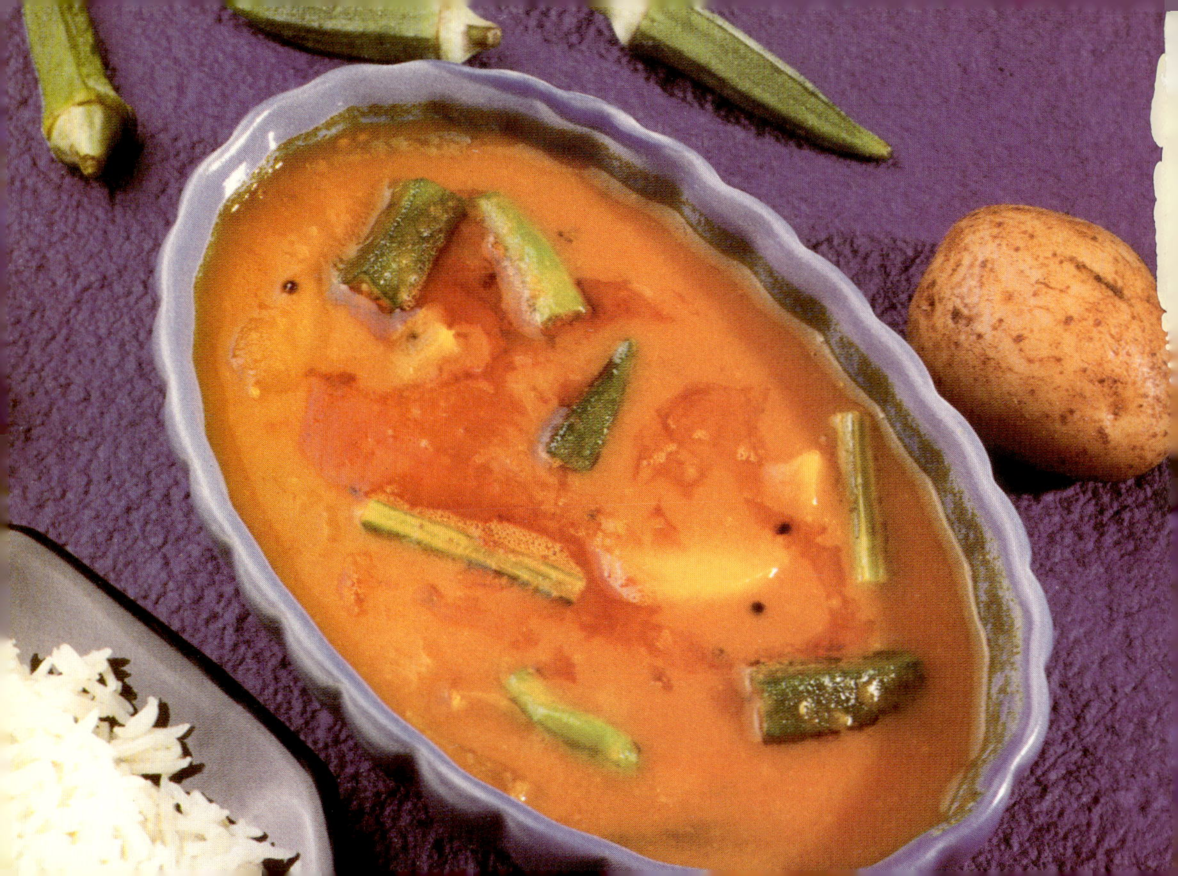

1. Boil tomatoes in 4 cups water for 3-4 minutes. Peel and puree in a mixer. Keep aside.
2. Heat 3 tbsp oil in a saucepan. Add rai and jeera. Add besan and roast over medium flame for 4-5 minutes till golden brown. Remove from heat. Add tomatoes and 4 cups of water.
3. Mix well. Heat again. When it begins to boil add all vegetables except lady's fingers.
4. Add haldi, red chillies and 2 cups water. Simmer for 10 min. Add kokums or tamarind pulp and boil for 5 minutes. Add salt, fried lady's fingers and coriander leaves. Serve.

Rice Breads & Raita

Nan

Nans are oblong flat breads traditionally baked in a clay oven, tandoor, *but I have made them in an electric oven with equal success.*

Serves 4

2 cups (200 gm) plain flour (*maida*)

½ tsp baking soda (*mitha soda*)

½ tsp salt

½ tsp baking powder

½ cup hot milk

½ cup warm water, or as required

1 tsp onion seeds (*kalaunji*) or 1 tsp black or white sesame seeds (*til*)

1. Sift the flour, baking soda and salt together in a bowl.
2. Mix the baking powder into the hot milk and keep aside, undisturbed, for 1 minute. Bubbles will start appearing on the surface.

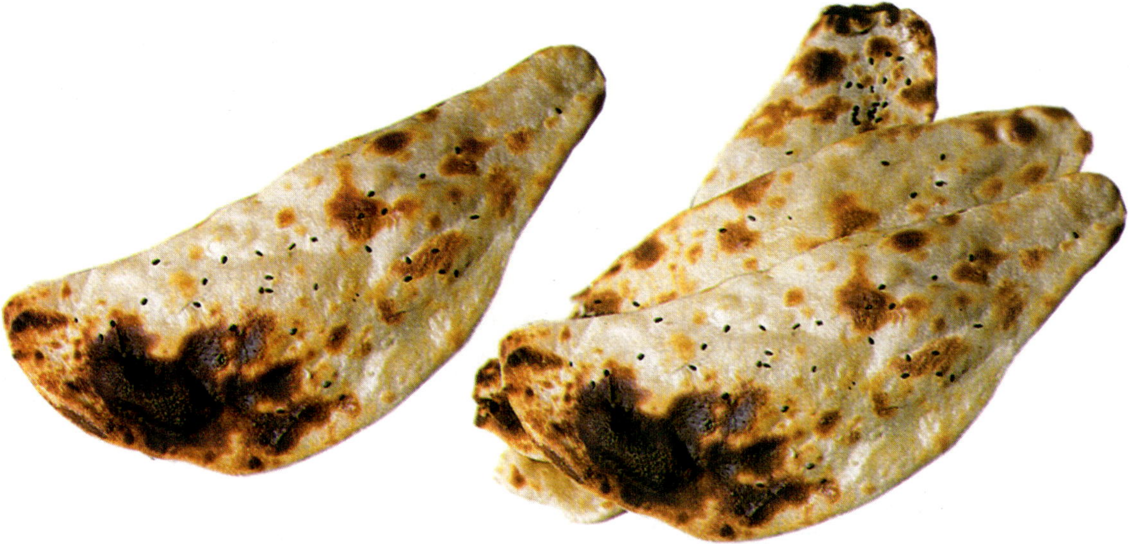

3. Add the milk to the flour and mix well. Knead, adding water, to make a soft dough. Continue to knead till the dough becomes smooth and elastic. Keep covered in a warm place for 3-4 hours to rise.
4. When it is time to serve the nans, divide the dough into 6-8 balls. Roll out each ball to an oblong shape. Sprinkle some nigella or sesame seeds and press them down with the rolling pin. Pull one side of the nan to give it the traditional pointed shape.
5. Apply some water on the back of the nan and press it on the walls of a hot tandoor. Alternately, cover the rack of the oven with aluminium foil and place the nans on it. Bake them in a very hot oven. When light brown spots appear on the surface, turn the nans and cook till done. Smear some butter on the hot nans and serve with dals or curries.

Jalpari Biryani

Serves 4

125 gm bhein or lotus stem (*kamal kakri*)
1 cup basmati rice - soaked for 20-30 minutes, ½ tsp salt, 4 cups water
3-4 green cardamoms (*chhoti elaichi*)
1 black cardamom (*moti elaichi*), ½" stick cinnamon (*dalchini*)

MINT PASTE (GRIND TOGETHER)
2-3 tbsp mint leaves (*poodina*), 4 tbsp coriander chopped, 1 green chilli

MASALA
3 onions, 1" piece ginger, ½ tsp red chilli powder, 1 tbsp raisin (*kishmish*)
½ cup curd (*dahi*) - well beaten & mixed with ¼ cup water

OTHER INGREDIENTS
2 tbsp chopped mint leaves (*poodina*)
2 onions - sliced and deep fried till brown
½ cup curd (*dahi*) - well beaten, 2 pinches of mace (*javitri*) - crushed and powdered
seeds of 2 green cardamoms (*chhoti elaichi*) - powdered

1. Peel bhein. Cut into thin diagonal slices and soak slices in water. Keep aside.
2. Prepare mint paste by grinding all the ingredients of the paste together.
3. Grind onions, ginger and red chilli powder together to a paste.
4. Heat 1 karchhi (4-5 tbsp oil) in a handi or a heavy bottomed pan. Add the onion paste. Cook on low flame till light brown and oil separates.
5. Add kishmish and stir for ½ a minute.
6. Reduce flame. Add beaten curd mixed with a little water, stirring continuously to prevent curd from curdling. Stir till masala turns thick.
7. Drain bhein and add to the masala. Add 1 tsp salt. Bhuno for 4-5 minutes.
8. Add 1 cup water. Cover with a tight fitting lid and cook on low flame for 15 minutes or till soft. The bhein should not taste raw, although it may taste a little hard.
9. Add mint paste. Bhuno for 5-7 minutes, remove from fire and keep aside. Keep bhein aside.
10. To prepare the rice, boil 4 cups water with all the saboot garam masala and salt.
11. Drain the soaked rice & add to boiling water. Keep checking & feeling a grain of rice in between the finger & thumb to see if it is done. Boil on medium flame for 7-8 minutes till the rice is nearly done. Take care to see that the rice is not over cooked.

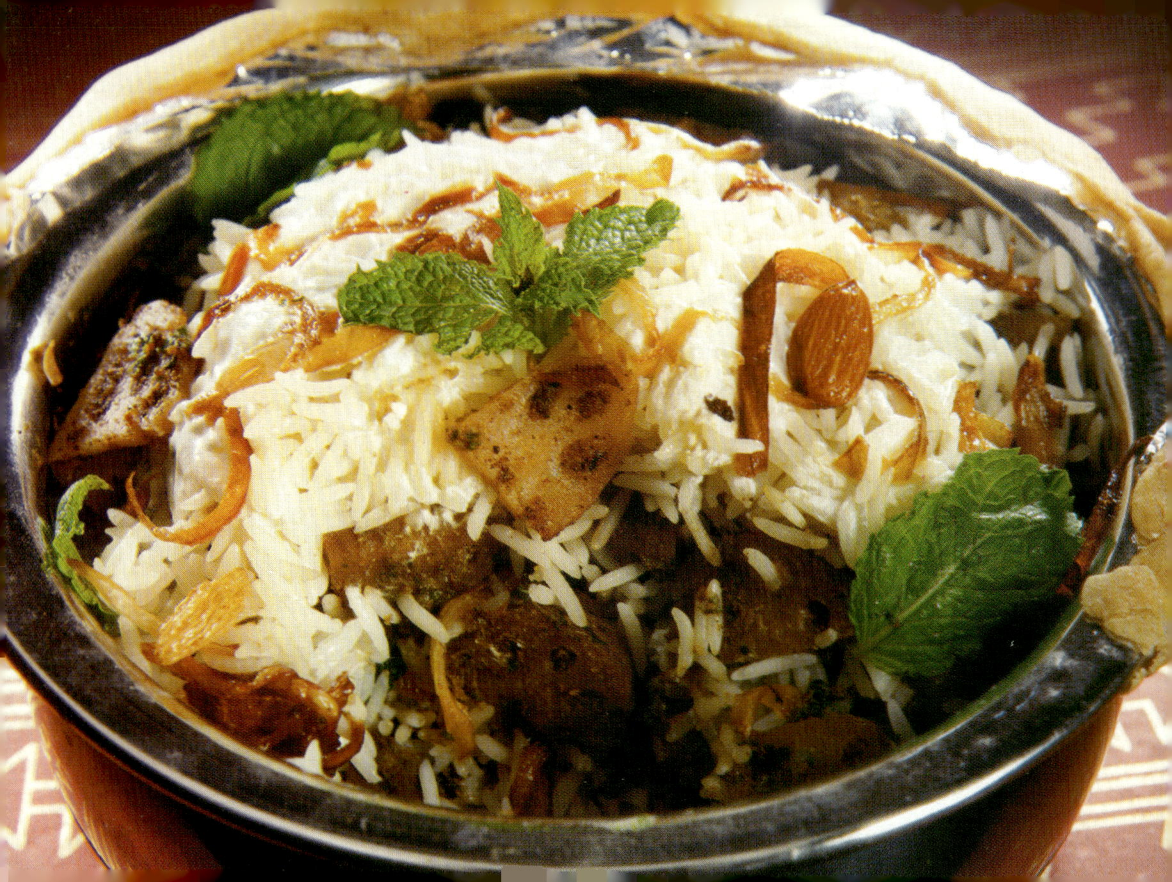

12. Strain rice in a rice strainer or colander. Keep aside uncovered for 10 minutes. Then spread the rice in a big tray.
13. Deep fry 2 sliced onions to a crisp brown colour. Keep aside.
14. Beat ½ cup curd. Add crushed and powdered javitri and chhoti elaichi to the curd. Keep aside.
15. Finely chop 2 tbsp mint leaves and keep aside.
16. To assemble the biryani, put half the vegetable with the masala in a handi.
17. Spread half the rice over it.
18. Spoon half the flavoured curd over it.
19. Sprinkle some fried onions and chopped mint leaves.
20. Repeat the masala vegetable and the other layers.
21. Cover the handi. Seal with atta dough and keep on dum for 15-20 minutes in a slow oven (100°C). Break the seal just before serving.

Lachha Poodina Parantha

The flavour of mint is crusted right on top of this so-easy-to-make flaky parantha, making every bite a pure delight!

Makes 6

4 tbsp freshly chopped or dry mint leaves (*poodina*), 2 cups whole wheat flour (*atta*)
1 tsp carom seeds (*ajwain*), 2 tbsp oil, ½ tsp salt, ½ tsp red chilli powder

1. Mix atta with all ingredients except poodina. Add enough water to make a dough of rolling consistency.
2. Make walnut-sized balls. Roll out to make a thick chappati.
3. Spread 1 tsp of ghee all over. Cut a slit from the outer edge till the centre.
4. Start rolling from the slit to form a cone.
5. Keeping the cone upright, press cone gently.
6. Roll out to a thick roti. Sprinkle poodina. Press with the belan (rolling pin).
7. Cook on a *tawa*, frying on both sides or apply some water on the back side of the parantha and stick it in a hot tandoor. Serve hot.

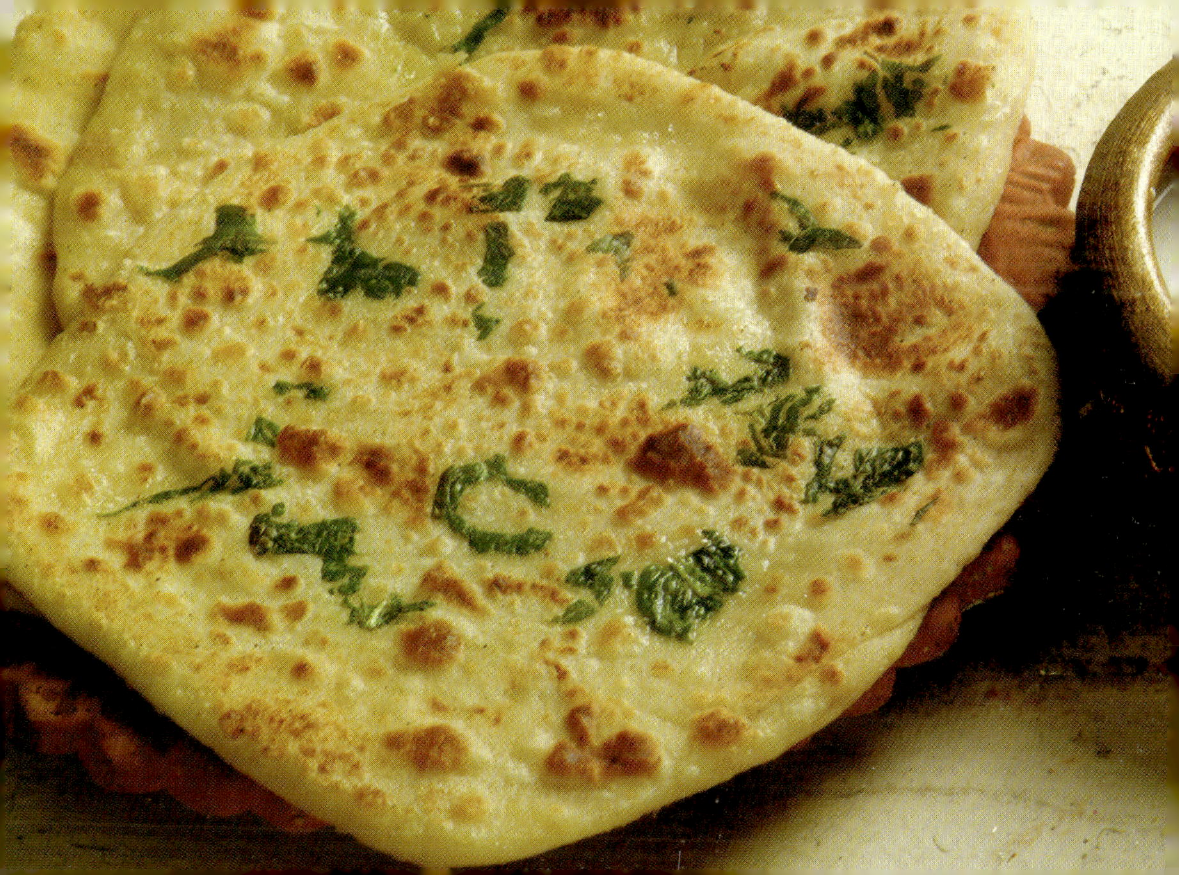

Southern Tomato Rice

Cooked rice is tossed in a spicy tomato base till it soaks up all the flavours.

Makes 6

1 cup basmati rice
4 small tomatoes - ground to a puree in a mixi
2-3 onions - chopped
¼ tsp turmeric (*haldi*) powder
1½ tsp salt or to taste
1 tsp red chilli powder
¼ tsp asafoetida (*hing*) powder

TEMPERING (*CHOWNK*)
3 tbsp oil
1 tsp mustard seeds (*sarson*)
1 tbsp gram lentils (*channe ki dal*)
few curry leaves

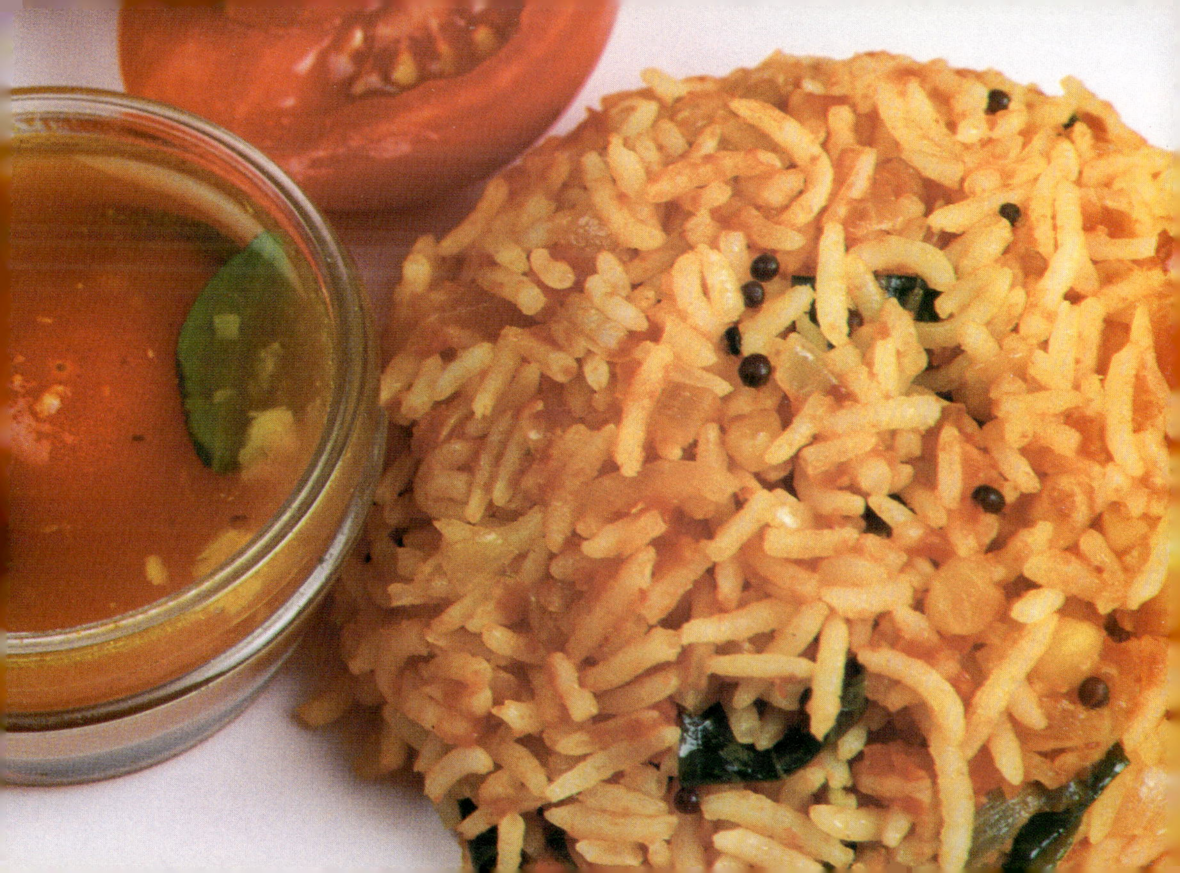

1. Clean & wash rice. Boil 5-6 cups water in a large pan. Add rice. Cook till done.
2. Strain the rice in a colander (big metal strainer). Keep aside to cool by spreading the rice in a big tray.
3. Heat oil in a *kadhai*. Reduce flame. Add hing powder. Add sarson & dal. Cook on very low flame till dal changes colour.
4. Add curry leaves & onions. Fry till onions turn light brown.
5. Add tomato puree.
6. Add haldi, salt & red chilli powder.
7. Cook on low flame till the dal turns soft & the tomatoes turn absolutely dry & oil separates.
8. Separate the rice grains with a fork & add to the tomatoes. Stir carefully till well mixed. Serve hot.

Baingan ka Raita

Cool and pure yogurt is contrasted with tingling mustard seeds, curry leaves and red chillies – with slices of fried brinjals stirred in, this makes the perfect raita.

Makes 4-6

1 small thin, long aubergine (*baingan*)
1 tsp chaat masala
2 cups yogurt (*dahi*)
1 tsp salt, oil to shallow fry

FOR TEMPERING (*TADKA*)
1 tbsp oil
1 tbsp black mustard (*sarson*) seeds
6-8 curry leaves (*curry patta*)
2 whole dry red chillies (*saboot sookhi lal mirch*)

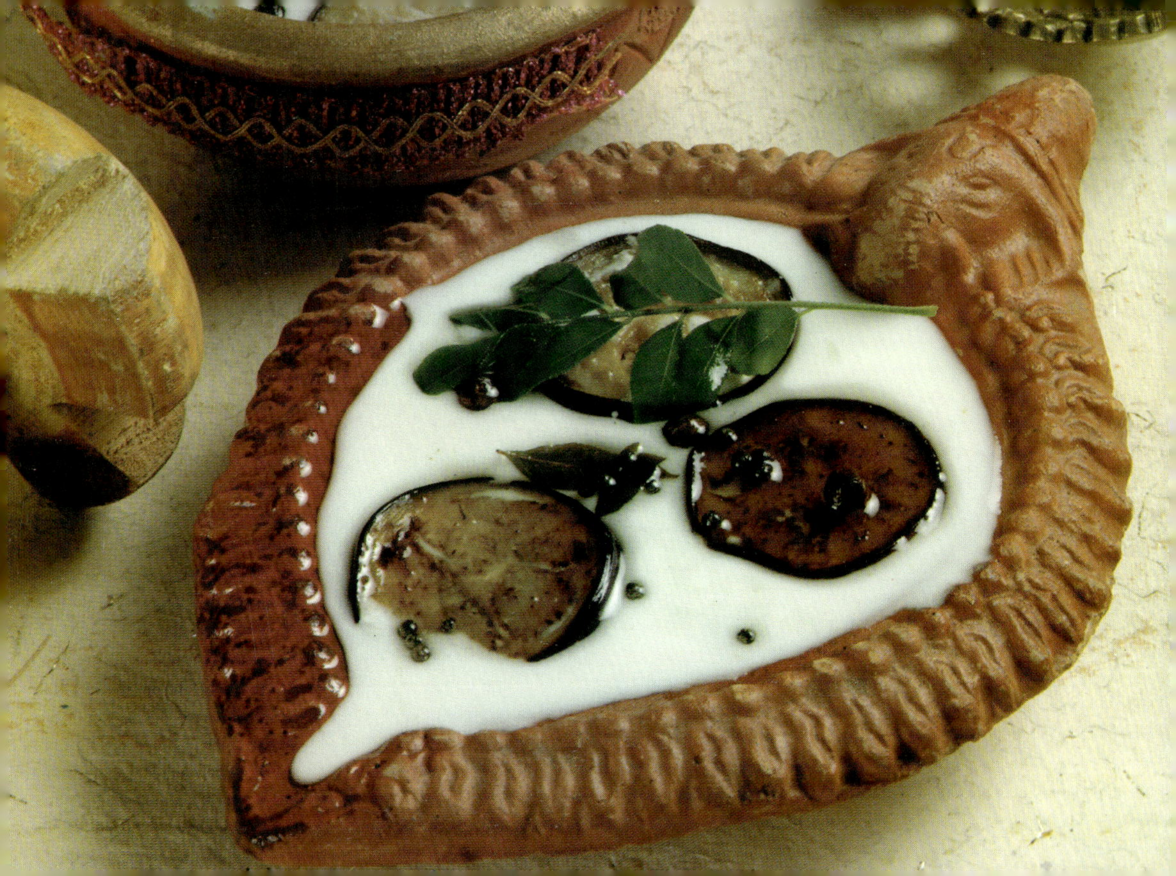

1. Wash and cut the baingan into thin round slices.
2. Heat the oil in a non stick frying pan; add baingan, fry till light brown. Sprinkle chaat masala. Remove.
3. Beat dahi with salt. Pour into a serving bowl. Add baingan. Mix gently.
4. For the tempering, heat the oil and all ingredients of the tadka, wait for a minute. Immediately pour over the yogurt. Serve chilled.

Beetroot Raita

We have used beetroot in our raita, believe me it's delicious.

Serves 3

1 cup (250 gms) yogurt (*dahi*)
½ of a small beetroot - boiled, peeled & grated
½ tsp roasted cumin (*bhuna jeera*) powder
a pinch of red chilli powder
a pinch of salt, ½ tsp sugar

1. Beat yogurt till smooth. Add jeera, chilli powder, salt and sugar. Mix.
2. Add just enough beet to get a nice pink colour. Check taste. Serve chilled.

Desserts

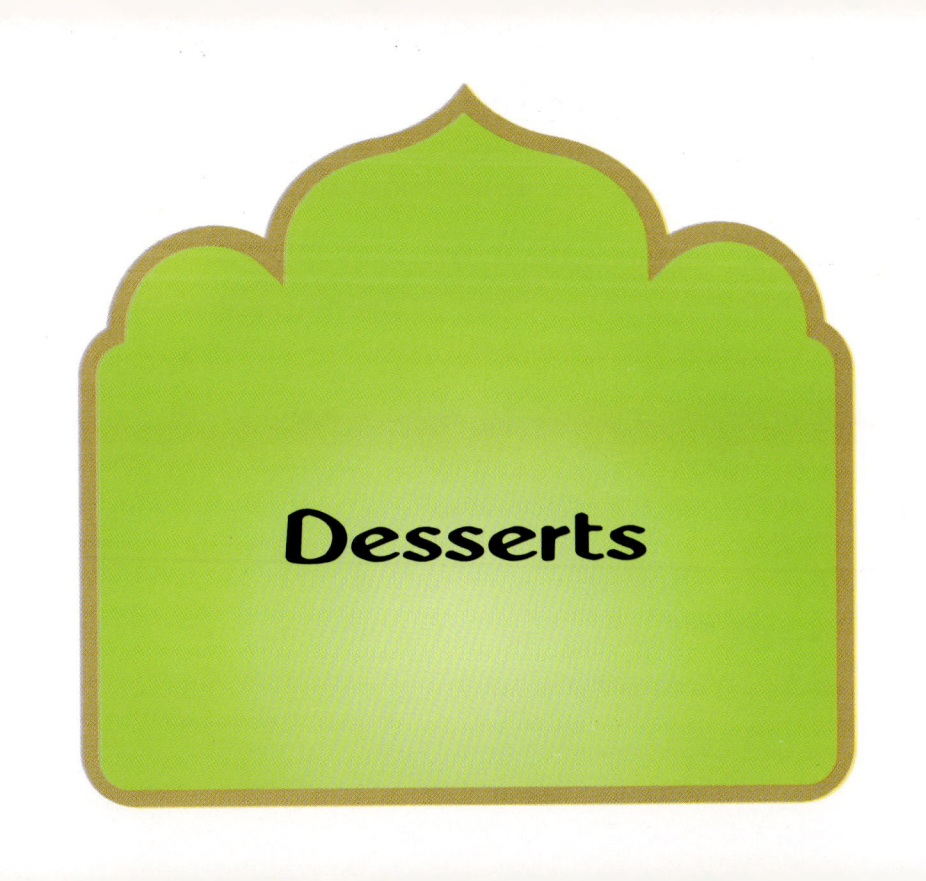

Pista Kesar Kulfi

The delicious Indian Ice cream topped with sweetened thin vermicelli. Saffron lends it's flavour and colour to this most popular Indian dessert. Pistachios & almonds add to the richness.

Serves 6-8

1 kg full cream milk

5 tbsp skimmed milk powder

3 tbsp cornflour

¼ cup sugar

6-7 strands saffron *(kesar)*

3-4 green cardamoms *(chhoti elaichi)* - crushed

1 tbsp shredded pistachios *(pista)*, 1 tbsp shredded almonds *(badam)*

FALOODA

1 cup thin rice vermicelli

3-4 strands saffron *(kesar)*

3 tbsp sugar

2 green cardamoms *(chhoti elaichi)*

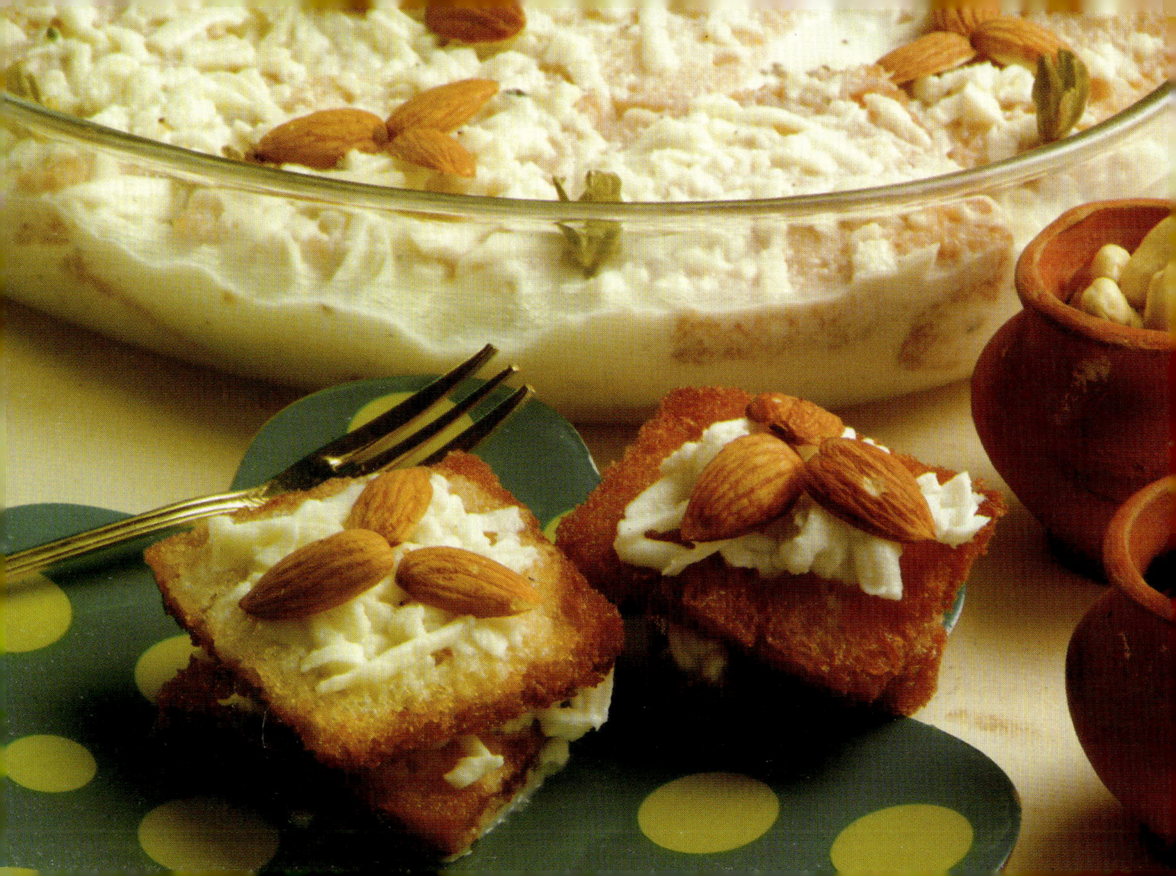

Shahi Tukri Lajawaab

In this innovative interpretation of a traditional dessert, fried bread is soaked in a mixture of sweetened, thickened milk cooked with grated paneer.

Serves 8-10

6 slices of bread - sides removed & each cut into 4 pieces & deep fried till golden brown
5 tbsp of chopped mixed nuts (*badaam, kishmish, pista* etc.), ¾ cup cold milk

PANEER LAYER
4 cups milk, ¾ cup sugar
¾ tsp green cardamom (*chhoti elaichi*) powdered
8 tsp cornflour dissolved in ½ cup milk
100 gm cottage cheese (*paneer*) - grated
2 drops of *kewra* essence

1. For the paneer layer, boil 4 cups milk. Simmer on low flame for 20 minutes.
2. In the meanwhile, boil sugar with ½ cup water in a separate pan. Keep on low heat for 5 minutes. Add grated paneer. Cook for 1 minute. Remove from fire.

1. Dissolve cornflour and milk powder in ½ cup milk to a paste. Heat the rest of the milk with sugar and kesar. Add the paste gradually, stirring continuously. Mix well. Add crushed seeds of chhoti elaichi. Boil. Simmer on low heat, for about 15 minutes till slightly thick.
2. Cool. Add pistachios and almonds. Fill in clean kulfi moulds and leave to set in the freezer for 6-8 hours or overnight.
3. To prepare the falooda boil 4 cups water. Add the rice vermicelli. Boil. Simmer on low heat for 2-3 minutes till the vermicelli turns soft and no crunch remains. Strain. Add cold water to refresh. Strain again.
4. Make a sugar syrup by boiling ¾ cup water, 3 tbsp sugar, kesar and chhoti elaichi together. Simmer for a couple of minutes. Remove from heat and put in the boiled vermicelli. Keep soaked in sugar syrup, in the refrigerator, till serving time.
5. To serve, remove the kulfi from the mould, cut into two halves lengthways and top with some falooda (without the syrup). Serve.

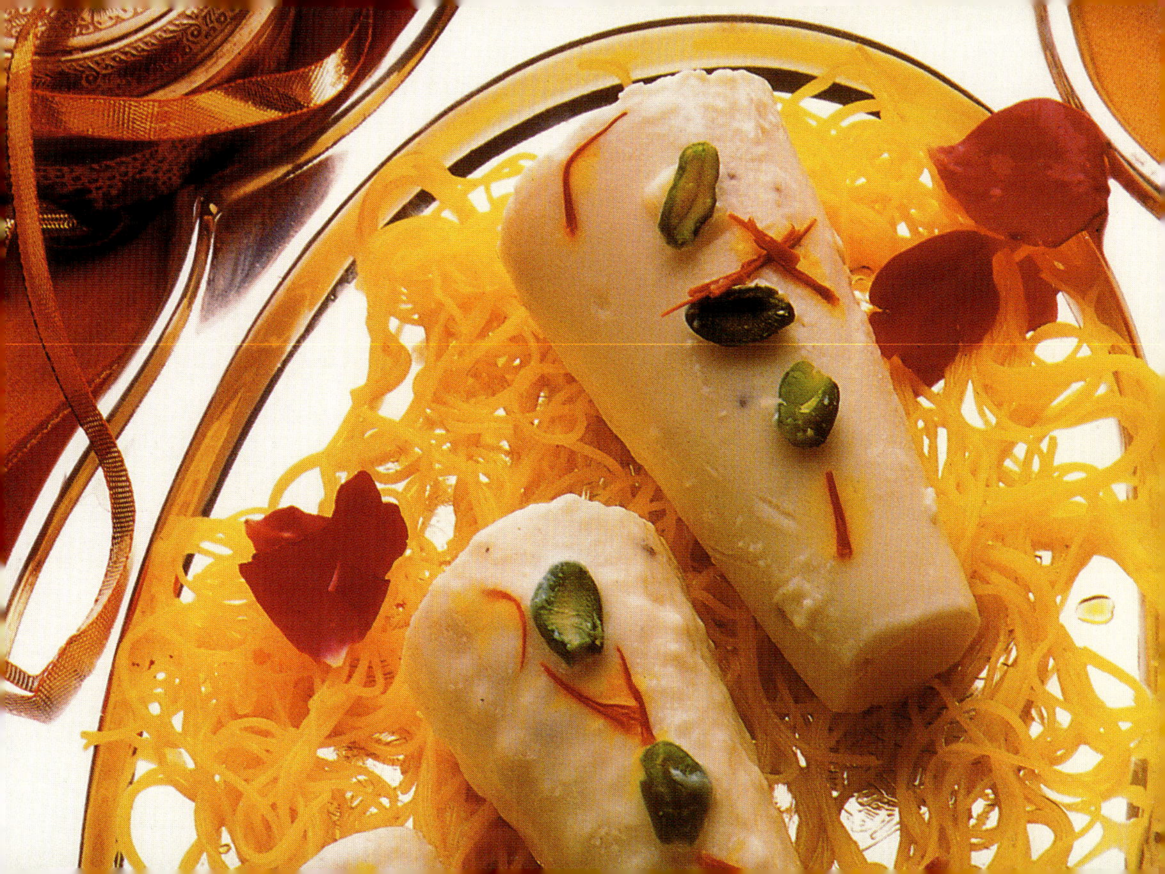

3. Add cornflour paste to the milk of step 1, stirring continuously. Keep stirring for 2 minutes till thick.
4. Add the prepared sugar and paneer mixture. Boil. Keep on heat for 1 minute. Remove from fire. Cool.
5. Add essence. Sprinkle elaichi powder. Keep aside.
6. Remove the side crusts of bread. Cut each slice into 4 square pieces. Heat oil in a *kadhai*. Deep fry each piece till golden brown. Let it cool.
7. Dip each piece of bread for a second in some cold milk, put in a small flat dish. Remove immediately.
8. Take a serving dish. Spread 1 tbsp of paneer layer at the bottom of the dish. Place pieces of fried bread together in a single layer to cover the base of the dish.
9. Spread about ½ tsp of the paneer mixture on each piece. Sprinkle 1 tbsp of chopped mixed nuts on the paneer.
10. Repeat the bread layer in the same way with bread pieces first then the paneer layer and finally topped with 1½ tbsp of chopped mixed nuts.
11. Repeat with the left over bread, paneer and nuts to get a 3 layered pudding. Cover with a cling wrap (plastic film) and let it set for at least ½ hour before serving. Serve at room temperature.

Malpuas

These pancakes are soaked in syrup, making them one of the best desserts for people with a sweet tooth. Prepare the batter at least one hour before frying the malpuas.

Gives 12-14 small malpuas

BATTER

1 cup flour (*maida*)

2 tbsp whole wheat flour (*atta*)

1 cup cream (*malai*)

½ cup milk (as much as required)

ghee for frying

SUGAR SYRUP

1 cup sugar, ½ cup water

a few strands saffron or 1-2 drops yellow food colour

1-2 green cardamoms (*chhoti elaichi*) - powdered

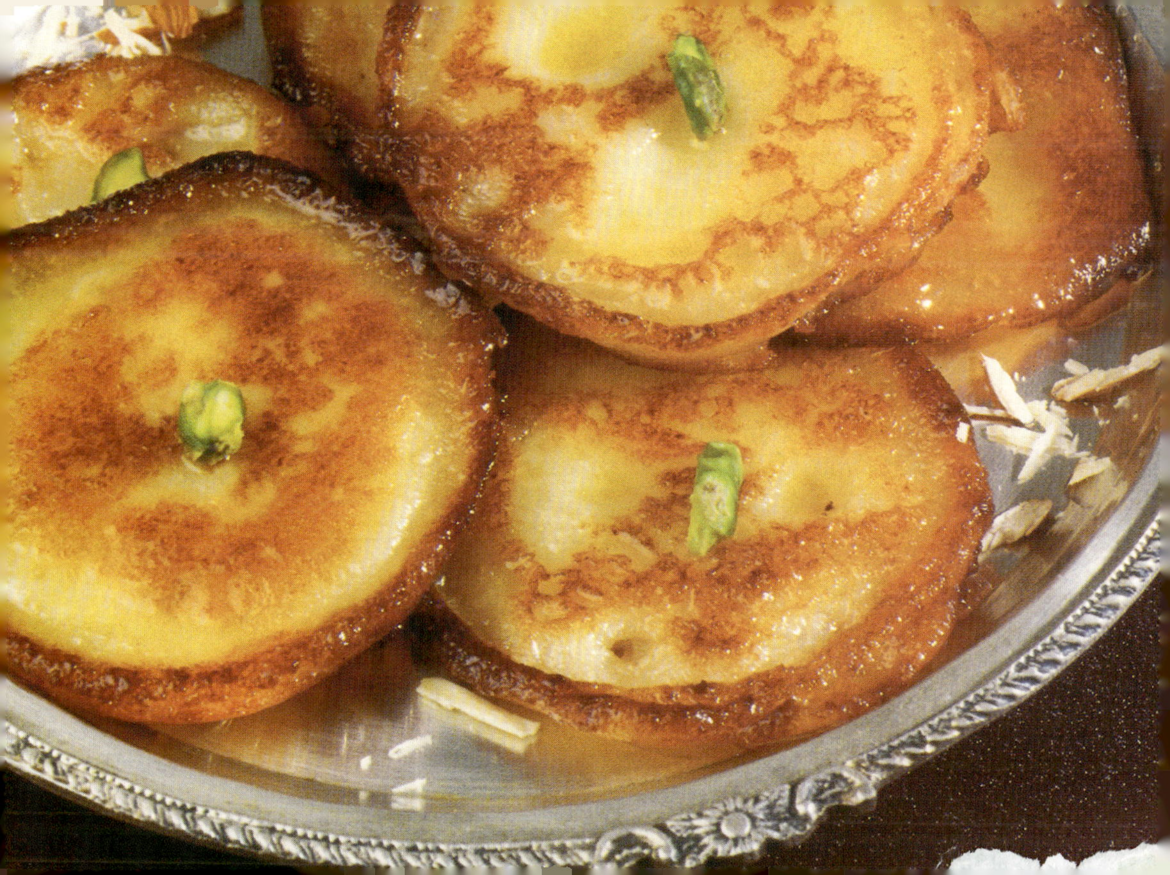

1. Mix all the ingredients well so that no lumps remain. The batter should be a little thicker than a cake batter. It should be of a soft dropping consistency. A thin batter will spread.
2. Leave aside for 1-2 hours. (very essential)
3. Heat ghee for deep frying in a nonstick frying pan.
4. With the help of a spoon drop a spoonful of batter in moderately hot ghee. Spread to get a small round malpua. Put as many (about 4-5) malpuas as the pan can hold.
5. Fry on both sides to golden brown. Drain and keep aside.
6. Mix sugar, water and all other ingredients for sugar syrup in a pan. Boil for 3-4 minutes to get one thread consistency syrup.
7. Drop malpuas in hot syrup, 2-3 at a time. Give 1-2 boils. Remove with a slotted spoon so that excess syrup is drained.
8. Place on a serving dish garnished with chopped almonds and pistas. Serve plain or with rabri or kheer.

Note: Malpuas can be fried in advance and kept without sugar syrup in an airtight box in the fridge for 1-2 days.

At the time of serving drop into hot sugar syrup, give 1-2 boils and serve hot.

Payasam

Fine vermicelli is cooked in ghee, sugar and milk then garnished with fried nuts & raisins.

Serves 6

4 cups milk
½ cup water
¾ cup sugar, or to taste
1 cup broken vermicelli (*seviyaan*)
2 tbsp *ghee*
a large pinch of saffron (*kesar*), optional
1 tbsp broken cashewnut pieces (*kaju tukda*)
2 tbsp raisins (*kishmish*)
3-4 cardamoms (*elaichi*) - powdered
a few drops rose essence

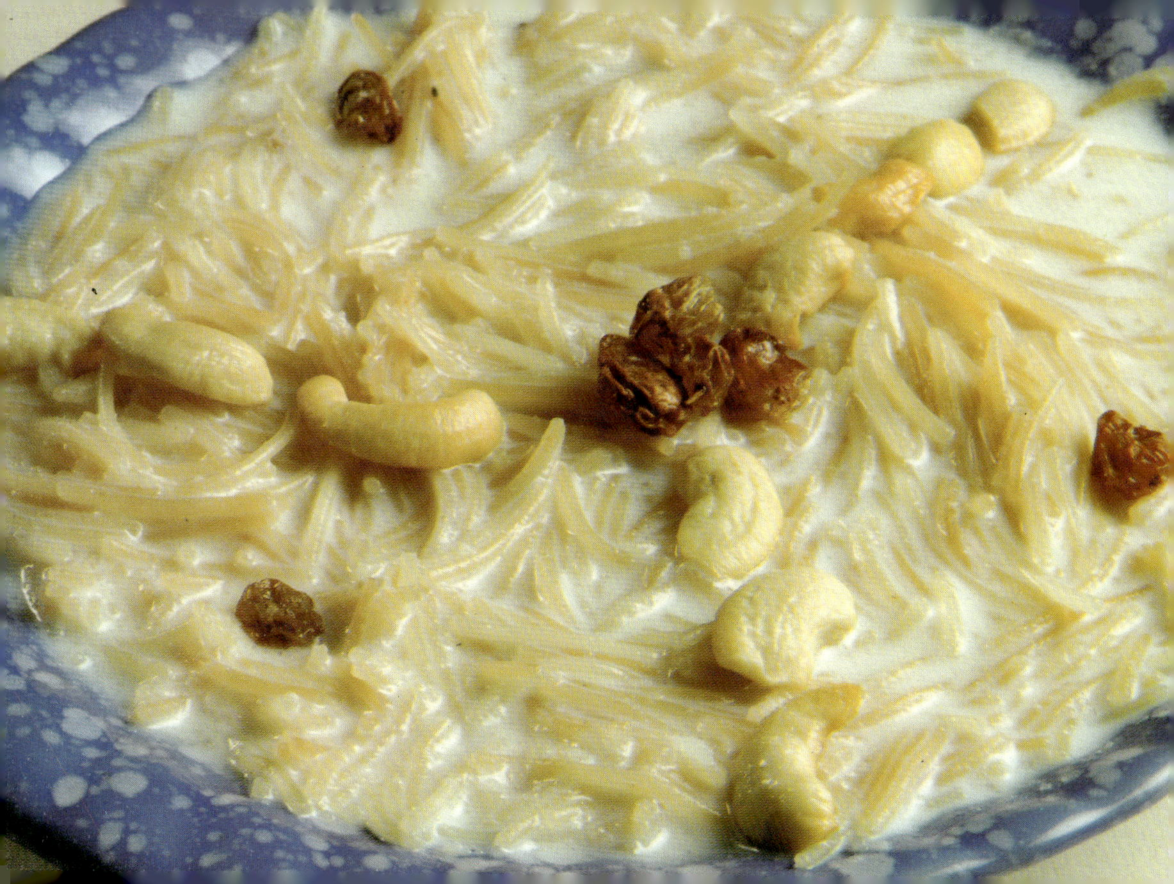

1. Heat ghee. Fry cashewnut pieces and raisins, remove, set aside.
2. Add seviyaan to the pan, fry to a light brown, add water, cook for just a minute, on low heat.
3. Now add the milk gradually, stirring.
4. Add sugar, continue to cook until payasam is quite thick. Remove from fire. Check sugar.
5. Add cardamom, nuts and raisins. Add rose essence, mix thoroughly. Serve hot or cold.

Note: You could add a large pinch of kesar along with milk while it is boiling, then omit rose essence.

Badaam ka Halwa

If you are looking for pure pleasure try this halwa! Almond paste and khoya sautéed in ghee, then cooked with sugar and milk.

Serves 4

150 gm (1 cup) almonds (*badam*), 200 gm *khoya* - grate or crumble, 1 cup sugar, 1 cup milk
15 gm (1 tbsp) clarified butter (*desi ghee*)
seeds of 2 green cardamoms (*chhoti elaichi*) - powdered

1. Soak almonds in water for 2-3 hours or overnight. Remove peel and grind to a paste. Keep almond paste aside.
2. Heat ghee in a heavy-bottom pan.
3. Add khoya, cook on low heat for about 4-5 minutes, till light golden.
4. Add almond paste cook for about 4-5 minutes, till khoya becomes golden.
5. Add sugar. Stir for 3-4 minutes on low flame.
6. Add milk and elaichi powder. Cook till halwa leaves ghee, approx. 10 minutes. Garnish with almonds.

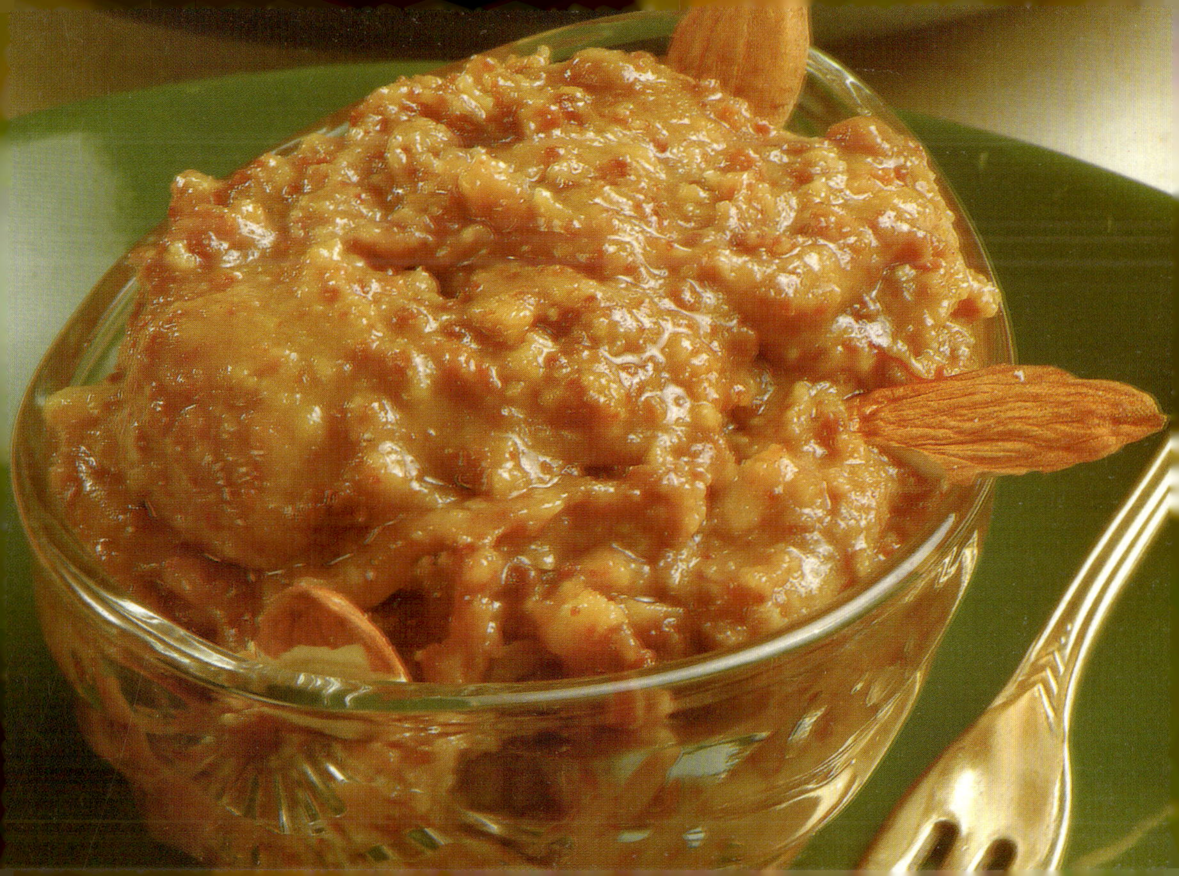

Glossary of Names/Terms

HINDI OR ENGLISH NAMES AS USED IN INDIA	ENGLISH NAMES AS USED IN USA/UK/OTHER COUNTRIES
Aloo	Potatoes
Badaam	Almonds
Basmati rice	Fragrant Indian rice
Capsicum	Bell peppers
Chaawal, Chawal	Rice
Choti Elaichi	Green cardamom
Chilli powder	Red chilli powder, Cayenne pepper
Cornflour	Cornstarch
Coriander, fresh	Cilantro
Cream	Whipping cream
Dalchini	Cinnamon
Degi Mirch, Kashmiri Mirch	Paprika
Elaichi	Cardamom
Gajar	Carrots
Gobhi	Cauliflower
Hara Dhania	Cilantro/fresh or green coriander

Hari Mirch	Green hot peppers, green chillies, serrano peppers
Jeera Powder	Ground cumin seeds
Kaju	Cashewnuts
Khumb	Mushrooms
Kishmish	Raisins
Maida	All purpose flour, Plain flour
Makai, Makki	Corn
Matar	Peas
Mitha soda	Baking soda
Nimbu	Lemon
Paneer	Home made cheese made by curdling milk with vinegar or lemon juice. Fresh home made ricotta cheese can be substituted.
Pyaz, pyaaz	Onions
Red Chilli Flakes	Red pepper flakes
Saboot Kali Mirch	Pepper corns
Saunf	Fennel
Soda bicarb	Baking soda
Spring Onions	Green onions, Scallions
Suji	Semolina
Til	Sesame seeds
Toned Milk	Milk with 1% fat content

INTERNATIONAL CONVERSION GUIDE

These are not exact equivalents; they've been rounded-off to make measuring easier.

WEIGHTS & MEASURES

METRIC	IMPERIAL
15 g	½ oz
30 g	1 oz
60 g	2 oz
90 g	3 oz
125 g	4 oz (¼ lb)
155 g	5 oz
185 g	6 oz
220 g	7 oz
250 g	8 oz (½ lb)
280 g	9 oz
315 g	10 oz
345 g	11 oz
375 g	12 oz (¾ lb)
410 g	13 oz
440 g	14 oz
470 g	15 oz
500 g	16 oz (1 lb)
750 g	24 oz (1½ lb)
1 kg	30 oz (2 lb)

LIQUID MEASURES

METRIC	IMPERIAL
30 ml	1 fluid oz
60 ml	2 fluid oz
100 ml	3 fluid oz
125 ml	4 fluid oz
150 ml	5 fluid oz (¼ pint/1 gill)
190 ml	6 fluid oz
250 ml	8 fluid oz
300 ml	10 fluid oz (½ pint)
500 ml	16 fluid oz
600 ml	20 fluid oz (1 pint)
1000 ml	1¾ pints

CUPS & SPOON MEASURES

METRIC	IMPERIAL
1 ml	¼ tsp
2 ml	½ tsp
5 ml	1 tsp
15 ml	1 tbsp
60 ml	¼ cup
125 ml	½ cup
250 ml	1 cup

HELPFUL MEASURES

METRIC	IMPERIAL
3 mm	1/8 in
6 mm	¼ in
1 cm	½ in
2 cm	¾ in
2.5 cm	1 in
5 cm	2 in
6 cm	2½ in
8 cm	3 in
10 cm	4 in
13 cm	5 in
15 cm	6 in
18 cm	7 in
20 cm	8 in
23 cm	9 in
25 cm	10 in
28 cm	11 in
30 cm	12 in (1 ft)

Nita Mehta's NEW RELEASES

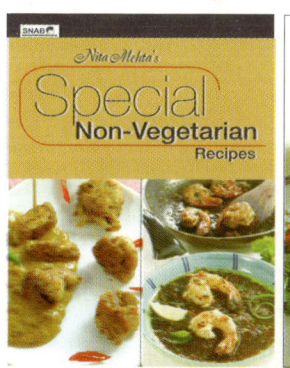

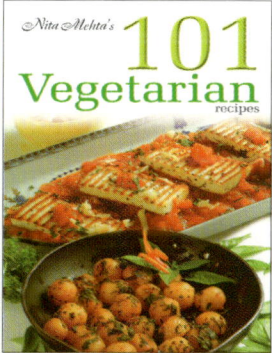

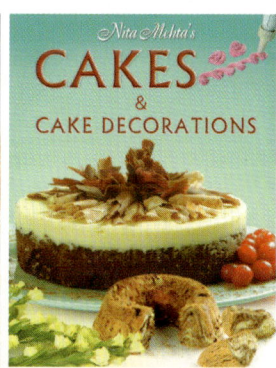

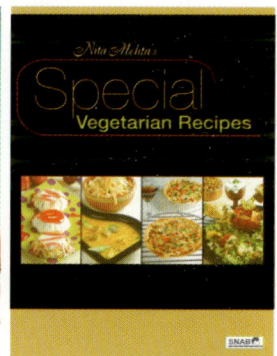

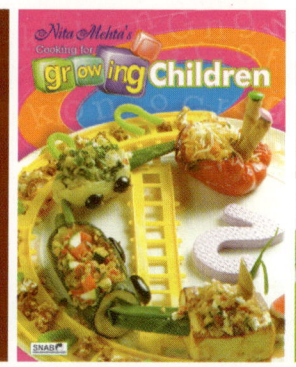

Nita Mehta's NEW RELEASES

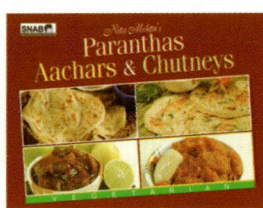

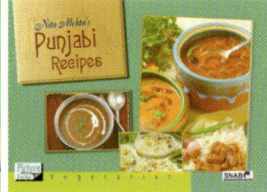

Nita Mehta's BEST SELLERS (Vegetarian)

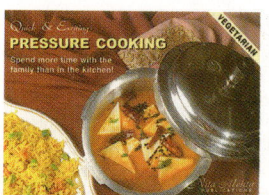

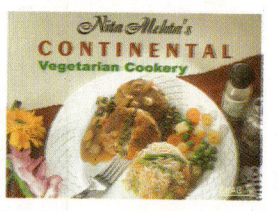

- Nita Mehta's All Time Favourite SNACKS
- Nita Mehta's Cakes & Chocolates
- Nita Mehta's Soups Salads & Starters
- Nita Mehta's Green Vegetables
- Nita Mehta's Vegetarian Soups
- Quick & Everyday PRESSURE COOKING
- Nita Mehta's Taste of GUJARAT
- Nita Mehta's Delicious ZERO OIL Cookbook
- Nita Mehta's PASTA & CORN
- Nita Mehta's Vegetarian Sandwiches
- Nita Mehta's PARTY FOOD
- Nita Mehta's CONTINENTAL Vegetarian Cookery

Nita Mehta's NEW RELEASES

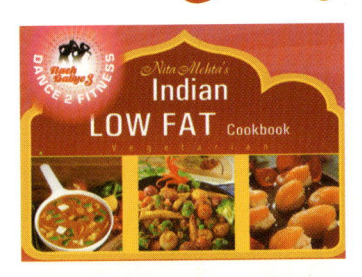

- Nita Mehta's Indian LOW FAT Cookbook
- Nita Mehta's Lose Weight
- Nita Mehta's Zero Oil Recipes
- Nita Mehta's Low Calorie SNACKS
- Nita Mehta's Stay Slim... Eat Right

COOKBOOK • Nach Baliye 3 • DANCE 2 FITNESS

In association with STAR TV